ANY DANGER OF GETTING A CUP OF TEA?

To Raymond,

ANY DANGER OF GETTING A CUP OF TEA?

by

Annette June Montemurro

Stoney Creek Publishing
Coquitlam
British Columbia
Canada

National Library of Canada Cataloguing in Publication

Montemurro, Annette June, 1930 -
Any danger of getting a cup of tea?

ISBN 0-9730982-0-1

1. Coppard, Edward. 2. World War, 1939-1945--Personal narratives, British. I. Title.
D811.C595 2002 940.54'8141 C2002-910623-0

Printed in Canada by Ward Printing
Vancouver
British Columbia

Stoney Creek Publishing
915 North Road
Coquitlam, B.C.
V3J 1P9

website: www.stoneycreekpublishingbc.com
e-mail: stonycrk@telus.net
phone: 604-936-1696
fax: 604-936-9884

Too often oral history is lost forever when the narrator dies but I was fortunate in being able to record many of my father's recollections.

Over the years I had, of course, heard many of Dad's engaging stories but it was not until he was seventy that he first talked about the most traumatic event of his life. He was with my sister and me one day as we watched our children celebrating my daughter's tenth birthday.

Dad suddenly said, "I was ten when I watched my mother choke to death in front of me. It was the worst day of my life."

We listened as Dad talked and talked and then we put a tape recorder in front of him.

Acknowledgements

In writing this book I have been in touch with several members of the Coppard clan whose stories about the family have been included. I would like to thank the following people: Sandra and Gary Coppard, Bobby Coppard, Brian Coppard, Douglas Coppard, Clare Coxall and Helen Hamilton.

Thanks especially to Jennifer Hargreaves who fielded numerous phone calls and put me in touch with Local History Librarians who were unfailingly helpful.

A special thank you goes to John Coppard who researched the family tree and furnished me with information about the Georges.

I am very grateful to Tom Lawrence who contributed accounts of balloon barrage deployment in the Firth of Forth and supplied me with a wealth of information.

I am indebted to Greg Moon who instructed me about the history of the marathon race, Olive Smith who added to accounts of wartime in West Wickham, and Helen Clement who verified dates of birth of the Lewes Coppards.

Rosanne and Ralph Montemurro have been enthusiastic supporters of my endeavour. Ralph read the text from the perspective of a grandson and I appreciate his helpful comments.

I am grateful to Eileen Kernaghan and members of the Port Moody Writers' Group who read the manuscript and encouraged me to publish.

Lastly a big thank you to Frank Montemurro who logged countless hours at the computer and put golf on hold until the project was completed.

Contents

SCHOOL DAYS

***My** best asset in those days was a pair of strong, fleet young legs. I got out of a lot of trouble that way.*

"Name?"
"Coppard, Ma'am."
"First name?"
"Edward, Ma'am."
"Middle name? "
"Haven't got one, Ma'am."
"Everyone has one! "

Even a timorous five-year-old knows how many names he has. Edward Coppard - thirteen letters in all. This lack of a middle name was to elicit comment and questions throughout his life.

Edward started school when he was five, in 1910. On the first day, his younger sister, Dorothy, upset at losing her playmate, was allowed to accompany him partway. There was a special bond between the two youngest children in the family.

"Let me carry your satchel, Edward."

She threaded her arms through the loops and Edward adjusted the satchel. His sister trotted on her short, stocky little legs beside Edward, the satchel bouncing on her back. She was proud of him in his new school clothes: short grey trousers, white shirt, black blazer and cap. His shoes were brightly polished. He looked apprehensive and his big, green eyes blinked constantly. At the end of the street Dorothy took off the satchel and handed it to him.

"Goodbye, Edward."

She kissed him.

"Sweethearts, sweethearts!" called out a boy riding by on his bike.

Edward's first term at school was difficult. He did not seem capable of learning anything and he was miserable. Then it was discovered that he was extremely short-sighted. How is a five-year-old to know that the fuzzy image he perceives is not what everyone else sees? Once he had his glasses, the blur on the blackboard came into focus and he began to succeed.

At the age of seven, boys and girls were segregated by sex and Edward went to Melvin Road Boys' School where he stayed until he left school at fourteen. Students walked through the asphalt schoolyard to the red brick school building. Inside, the cramped classrooms were hardly inviting. A tall man could see little out of the high windows; a boy seated at a desk could see nothing but the four walls.

The school was a rough one, over the railway bridge, literally 'on the wrong side of the tracks', but Edward usually managed to avoid trouble. He made sure that he was not around when the bullies were looking for a victim. If he was taken by surprise he could always outrun them.

There was one situation he was not able to avoid, however. At the age of ten he lost all his hair. World War I was in progress and while his father and uncles were away in the army, Edward and his sisters went often to Grandpapa's house to see him. Grandfather George Martin Coppard had a commanding presence. He was a big man with a bald, egg-shaped head. He wore a large walrus moustache. While

George always welcomed his grandchildren, they were afraid of him. He dominated the family and intimidated them with his unpredictable temper. He was given to sudden rages. Once when Edward's grandmother had not cooked fish to his liking, he shouted,

"This is like leather, woman. Cook me another fillet."

He had lifted his plate with the offending fish and thrown it against the wall.

While visiting their grandfather one day, the children learned that Uncle Bob, a favourite uncle, was home on leave from the trenches in France.

"Where's Uncle Bob?"

"He's out with Ronnie. But he'll be back soon."

While Katy and Dorothy stayed to talk to their grandfather, Edward and Connie went up to the attic, a long empty room where they often played games. Here they saw Bob's army gear and several old helmets. Each of them grabbed a helmet, put it on their head and pranced around the room. When they heard sounds of Bob's return, they ran downstairs to greet him.

"Where'd you get all these helmets, Uncle Bob?"

"They need fumigating. Take them off!"

But it was too late. Their heads became infested with ringworm and they were taken to a doctor who decided that they needed x-ray treatment. No one questioned the doctor. The children were used as guinea pigs in a new technology little understood.

In the office neither Edward nor Connie knew what to expect. They felt frightened.

"Are you going to shave our hair off?" asked Connie.

She voiced Edward's own fear.

"No, no, of course not. Come over here, boy!"

And Edward's head was zapped.

"Stand here, young lady."

Then Connie received the same treatment.

Within a week all their hair had fallen out. Connie's hair had been her pride: long, thick and black. She became hysterical and refused to leave the house until her hair grew in again. But Edward, as a boy, was expected to be made of sterner stuff. In absolute misery he went to school as usual. His teacher, Mr. Thomas, was understanding and allowed him to keep his cap on in class but Edward was fair game for the other boys. In the schoolyard he was constantly on the run from boys trying to snatch the cap off his head.

"Baldie!"

"Old man!"

The school inspector, Mr. Bradley, visited the school every month. When he entered the classroom, each boy stood to attention beside his desk. The inspector's eyes moved from boy to boy, judging, weighing, looking to find fault, while they waited. His eyes lighted on Edward.

"Boy, remove that cap!"

Edward's hands flew to his cap but he did not take it off.

"Boy!"

A steely look came over Edward's face. He was not used to being defiant. Although he was petrified of Mr. Bradley, he was determined to keep his cap on. Leaning towards the inspector, Mr. Thomas whispered in his ear. Mr. Bradley's gimlet eyes moved on to the next boy. When the inspector left the room Edward sank into his seat, trembling, still clutching the cap to his head.

It was months before Connie's and Edward's hair grew in again although never as fully as before. Each morning when he awoke Edward ran his hands over his head hoping that a miraculous growth had taken place overnight. Then he would go to the mirror and peer anxiously at his scalp to see if any hair had appeared. When finally a light fuzz had grown, he judged it to be sufficient to remove his cap in class.

Another far more traumatic event for Edward and his sisters occurred later that same year. Kathleen, the children's mother, died of tuberculosis. She had been sick for years and Aunt Constance came frequently to the house to help her ailing sister. After Kathleen had died and when the children's father, Ted, was away in the Army, she moved into the house to care for the family.

People were overtly unkind to mentally handicapped people. There was always someone in the neighbourhood known as the 'village idiot' who was fair game for taunts and abuse.

Robert, a big, ungainly man with vacant eyes lived in Beckenham Road. Sometimes as he walked down the street he would be surrounded by a group of boys who were deliberately impeding his progress.

"Nincompoop, nincompoop!" chanted one boy as he pushed him.

"Booby, booby!" yelled another as he planted himself in front of Robert, causing him almost to fall. Robert seemed never to take offense.

Having watched this for a while one day, Edward decided to join in the baiting. He gave Robert a little shove and was astonished when Robert turned around and came at him. Edward took off and quickly outpaced him. But he had underestimated Robert.

As Edward walked home from school next day Robert lay in wait for him with a potato sack. Robert grabbed him and stuffed him in the sack. Then Edward felt himself being whirled round and round. He was terrified and sickened by the smell of the soil in his nostrils. Eventually Robert tired of the sport and dropped the sack. Edward's head hit the ground with a sickening thud.

When the sound of Robert's footsteps had receded, Edward crawled out of the sack, weak and dizzy. His head hurt. Suddenly he realized that Robert was a real person. In spite of the fact that he looked different, Robert had feelings like everyone else. Ashamed of his own behaviour, Edward crept home and told no one what had happened.

Discipline at school was harsh but fair. Frank and Johnny, two boys in Edward's class, were often in trouble and Edward kept out of their way. One day Johnny was caned for bullying a younger child.

"I'll get my Dad up here to you!"

"Good," said the headmaster, "you tell your father I'll be delighted to see him!"

On his way home one day Edward saw that Frank and Johnny had grabbed James, one of his classmates. Frank was holding him down while Johnny was industriously rubbing horse manure into their unfortunate victim's hair. Edward felt sorry for James and would have liked to have gone to his rescue, but knew that he was no match for the two older boys together. However, there was never much excitement on Beckenham Road and this spectacle was not to be missed. He stood at a safe distance, watching James' discomfiture, waiting to see what happened.

James, goaded beyond endurance, suddenly threw off his tormentors and with a roar of rage came after Edward. Edward took to his heels and belted home. He vaulted over the garden gate, ran up the path and burst through the front door which was never locked. Aunt Constance was in the kitchen chopping vegetables for dinner. She came up the hall, knife in hand.

"What's the matter?"

Aunt Constance set great store by Edward, he being the only boy in the family. Butter wouldn't melt in his mouth.

"There's a boy," gasped Edward, "a boy chasing me."

"Good heavens, good heavens!"

Flourishing the knife, she reached the doorway just as James arrived. He was a sorry sight with torn clothes, clods of manure stuck in his hair and a filthy, tearstained face.

"Go away, boy, go away," said Aunt Constance. And she closed the door.

Edward left school at fourteen. His father wanted his help in the fish shop and was not interested in any suggestion that Edward be allowed to continue his education. And he had no mother to plead his cause. As far as it went, Melvin Road School did well by him, however. The standard of instruction was high within the confines of what was taught. In the top class, he came under the influence of an inspired, dedicated teacher. History was not just a list of dates to be memorized, but a discussion of the lives and actions of real people.

"Ask 'why?' Always ask 'why?'" admonished Mr. Hereford. "Question everything."

In literature, Mr. Hereford taught the boys not only the standard fare of Kipling's poem:

If you can keep your head about you when all about you
Are losing theirs and blaming it on you….

he also introduced them to Shelley, Yeats and Housman.

Edward could always call to mind the poetry he had learned by heart at school:

When I was one-and-twenty
I heard a wise men say
'Give crowns and pounds and guineas
But not your heart away;
Give pearls away and rubies

But keep your fancy free.'
But I was one-and twenty,
No use to talk to me.

When I was one-and-twenty
I heard him say again,
'The heart out of the bosom
Was never given in vain;
'Tis paid with sighs a plenty
And sold for endless rue.'
And I am two-and-twenty,
And oh, 'tis true, 'tis true.

Edward enjoyed the daily singing of folk and patriotic songs. He remembered all the songs he had sung:
The British Grenadiers, Heart of Oak, and Rule Britannia. He read avidly (Dickens was his favourite) and learned to savour the sound of words, the poetry of words. He knew an immense enjoyment of language which was to be further honed by the Cockneys with whom he worked. By the time he left school Edward had developed a passion for history and a love of literature which stayed with him all his life.

George Martin Coppard and family circa 1915

Back row: Frank(s.), unknown, George Maynard(s.), Edward(Ted)(s.), Katy(Ted's d.), Constance(Ted's 2nd w.), Robert(Bob)(s.);
Second row: Ethel(Frank's w.), Caroline(Chicksee)(George Maynard's w.), Emily(d), GEORGE MARTIN(Robert's d. on knee), Kathleen(d.), Mary(Robert's w.) d. on knee;
Front row: Connie(Ted's d.), Edward(Ted's s.), Dorothy(Ted's d.), Ruth(Herbert's w.), Herbert(Bert)(s.), Doris(Frank's d.), Geoffrey(Frank's s.).

Louie Anstey and family circa 1918

Back: Jack Webber (Louie's nephew)
Middle: Louie Anstey, Alice Anstey (daughter)
Front: Edwin Anstey (son).

GIRL NEXT DOOR

Alice was a holy terror. She was so repressed by her parents that she did crazy things. Aunt Constance used to lead her on because she got such a kick out of her antics. One day Alice surpassed herself and Papa banned her from the house.

The Coppards - Ted, Kathleen and their children Katy, Connie, Edward and Dorothy - lived in Avenue Road. The back door of their house opened into the kitchen to the side of which was the scullery. From the kitchen a passage led to the dining room on the left and the sitting room on the right. A staircase opposite the front door led to the three bedrooms, bathroom and toilet upstairs.

On the corner of the street was a bakery with a sweet-shop adjacent to it. Then there were the Anstey and Coppard houses, mirror images of each other. The Anstey family consisted of Charlie, Louie, and their daughter, Alice.

Alice Anstey was an only child until the birth of her brother when she was ten. She was a sickly child and was frequently away from school. Confined to her room upstairs by herself, she was often lonely. In the back yard of the sweet shop was an ice cream machine. From her bedroom she could hear the machine start up. She would run to her window and lean out to watch the activity. As soon as the machine stopped she rushed downstairs.

"Mother, Mother, the ice cream's ready. May I please have some money?"

She was always the first customer in the shop.

Alice Anstey and Dorothy Coppard used to walk the mile to school together, coming home for lunch each day. After Alice had eaten her lunch, her mother made her sit still for twenty minutes before she was allowed to start back to school.

"You must digest your food, Alice," admonished Louie.

Dorothy waited impatiently for her. As soon as Alice was allowed to leave she would walk decorously beside Dorothy to the corner of the street. Out of sight of Louie, however, the girls' demeanour changed. They ran, they skipped, they hopped. Alice would turn cartwheels, petticoats flying, to the consternation of passing neighbours.

Edward and his friend Ernie pranced down the street, holding hands and chanting:

Alla balla bingo
Like a dalla jingo
Like a jesta monger
Abba daba do
Abba daba moo
Like a jesta monger

A stream ran alongside Beckenham Road, where the children walked to and from school. Edward and his friends built dams in the stream and floated homemade boats in the lakes they created. Then an interfering adult would break up the dam and they had to start all over again.

There was always a current moving through the water trapped behind the dam. The boys launched their boats below the dam and would watch to see whose boat reached the end of the lake first.

"Let's have a go?" asked Alice.

"No. Girls aren't allowed," was Ernie's quick response.

"It's not fair. Boys have all the fun."

Edward would not have minded Alice and Dorothy being there. He was used to girls; he had three sisters. Alice envied the freedom which Edward and his sisters appeared to enjoy.

"Meanie! Edward's boat's winning anyway. I hope yours sinks!"

There was a shout and a big splash. In his effort to generate waves behind his boat, Edward had fallen in.

"Now you're for it, Edward."

Edward scrambled out of the ditch and ran home. It was a cold winter day and he was shivering. As he opened the door he encountered his father, home early from market. Papa stripped off Edward's clothes, and walloped him. He had to stay home from school that afternoon because he had no other clothes to put on.

The Coppards and Ansteys were good neighbours except in the matter of the rubbish bin. At the rear of the Coppard's back garden was a lane along which Charlie Anstey wheeled his bike every day on his way to and from work. The Coppard's rubbish bin, which should not have been there, was frequently in his way and he wrote to the landlord complaining about it. Unlike his neighbours, Charlie followed rules and regulations precisely. Everyone hated the landlord and Aunt Constance was outraged when the Coppards received a letter from him about the placement of their rubbish bin. Normally a mild-tempered person, she was very upset with Charlie. That evening she went to his house, formally, to the front door.

"Mr. Anstey," she said, (this was not the occasion for the familiar Charlie by which she normally addressed him) "I am not an unreasonable person. If you had told me that our rubbish bin was inconveniencing you, then it would have been moved. It was certainly not necessary to involve the landlord. I am very disappointed in you."

Charlie was dumbfounded by this outburst from the usually gentle Constance. She stalked away down the path before he could even begin to formulate a response.

Alice found the Coppard mènage easygoing and congenial. Kathleen was too sick to be involved in the children's activities but welcomed Alice with a weak smile whenever she came to play with Dorothy. Aunt Constance was at the house each day to help her sick sister and did not control Alice's every movement in the manner her own mother did. At home Alice was expected to be quiet and decorous. At the Coppards she could be as noisy as she liked except when Papa was there. Aunt Constance found Alice amusing and used to encourage her antics. Alice would never refuse a dare so Edward and Dorothy led her on.

"Bet you wouldn't ring all the doorbells on our street."

Alice was off.

"Mr. Grower saw me. He says he's going to tell my father. I don't care."

She was a hellion, a nuisance, but she had entertainment value.

Alice tried always to avoid Papa Coppard's attention. When she came in one day to play with Dorothy, Papa was in the sitting-room. Aunt Constance said,

"Dorothy's upstairs, Alice."

Upstairs, Alice found Dorothy having a bath in the huge tub. She stripped off her clothes and jumped in.

"Let's have more water," said Alice.

They filled the tub and then started sliding back and forth, back and forth, generating a huge wave. The water rose, hung poised in the air over the lip of the bath a split second and then cascaded onto the floor. In the sitting room below where Papa sat reading a great gush of water landed on his newspaper. Papa rushed to the foot of the stairs and bellowed,

"Dorothy, what the hell's going on?"

"Sorry, Papa, there's a bit of a mess in the bathroom. I'm cleaning it up."

Alice grabbed her clothes, ran to Dorothy's room and hurriedly dressed. She hid under Dorothy's bed until the fuss died down and then crept downstairs and out of the house.

Lighting in the house was provided by a gas fixture in the middle of the ceiling of each room. The kitchen was different, however, with light supplied from two wall fixtures. Each pipe extended horizontally from the wall for about eight inches and then turned at a ninety-degree angle upwards for a few inches. At the end of the pipe a mantle was lit, giving a good light.

Alice was often in the Coppard's kitchen, dancing around as Aunt Constance worked. Here she was not required to sit still. One day she jumped up and swung on one of the gas brackets. The pipe broke and gas started spewing into the room.

"Now you have done it. You'd better go home," said Aunt Constance as she ran to fetch Papa. Alice made a hasty exit.

"That girl is never to come into this house again!" roared Papa.

Kathleen (Gates) Coppard

Ted Coppard

Constance (Gates) Coppard

TUBERCULOSIS

I was playing with Dorothy, sitting at our mother's feet, and we were very happy. Then suddenly a great gush of blood came out of her mouth and she started choking. She died in front of us as we watched. It was the worst day of my life.

Tuberculosis ravaged Kathleen's family. In the early 1900s, to contract the disease was almost always a death sentence. There was no cure. It was the 1940s before an antibiotic became available to treat tuberculosis. How long a person survived depended on what form of the disease he or she developed. Victims of galloping consumption, as it was called, did not last long. Edward's Aunt Florrie, and Florrie and Norah, two of her three daughters, were all swept away in a few months.

When Kathleen married Ted in 1897, she herself must already have been harbouring the disease which would kill her, her son Thomas and her daughter Katy. Thomas, who was Kathleen and Ted's second child, died of tuberculous meningitis before he was a year old. This was a form of the disease which often attacked children.

Kathleen had been beautiful. Hers was a classic beauty - a perfect oval face, luminous brown eyes and a sweet mouth. She wore her soft, brown hair swept up above her forehead and drawn into a chignon at the nape of her neck. Kathleen did not die quickly as her nieces were to do. Hers was a slow death, a protracted dying.

As the disease advanced she developed a racking, persistent cough. She held a handkerchief to her mouth which was frequently stained with bright, arterial blood. She became emaciated and was perpetually exhausted and breathless as her lungs were eaten away.

As is often the case with children whose mothers are sick, her two youngest, Edward and Dorothy, were undemanding and became quite self-sufficient in each other's company. By the time Edward was ten, his mother was very weak. She could barely speak but liked to sit and watch Edward and Dorothy play.

On the day of her death Ted was at home. He hadn't gone for his usual long Sunday walk. Kathleen was very low in spirits but an occasional smile crossed her face as she sat in the rocking chair watching her children. They were seated on the floor at her feet playing a game of checkers. Dorothy won.

"What now, my darlings?" whispered Kathleen.

Edward and Dorothy turned to her.

"We're going…"

Suddenly a great gush of blood came out of her mouth and she started to choke. Edward ran to the door, flung it open and screamed,

"Papa! Papa!"

Ted rushed down the stairs and stood framed in the doorway, looking across at the tableau: two traumatized children and a dying woman.

"Now look what you've done to your mother!" yelled Ted.

He came over to Kathleen and spun the chair round. Her head fell back; she was struggling for breath. Ted looked at her with tears in his eyes and called to her,

"Kathleen, Kathleen!"

He did not realize that she was drowning in her own

blood.

Katy, back from an outing, came into the room.

"I'll get Louie."

She ran out. But by the time Louie Anstey, who was a nurse, arrived, Kate had ceased struggling. Louie looked at Kathleen, felt for a pulse, listened at her heart.

"She's gone, Ted. There's nothing anyone can do."

She gently wiped the blood from Kathleen's face. Tears streaming down his face, Ted carried his wife upstairs and laid her in their room. Edward and Dorothy were in shock; too traumatized to cry. They crept to bed and lay in each other's arms all night.

The next morning Edward woke with an overwhelming sense of sadness and loss. No one talked about feelings in those days but the memory of that terrible day was etched indelibly in Edward's mind; seared into his soul.

The day of the funeral, Edward and Dorothy, hand in hand, watched as their mother was lowered into the ground. Then, only then, could they believe that she was gone from them forever.

A few days later, a cousin of Kathleen's, a lady's companion, walked down the street to call on the family and express her condolences. She looked very like Kathleen. Edward and Dorothy were in the front garden, playing. As she approached the house, Dorothy screeched,

"It's Mama, it's Mama!"

Edward looked up. He thought it was his mother come back to life. Screaming, he and Dorothy ran indoors.

The children stayed home from school for a week. The morning of his first day back, Edward walked slowly, hesitantly, reluctant to face his classmates.

"I wonder what they'll do? What will they say? Will they laugh at me 'cause I feel so awful?"

But with the sensitivity which children sometimes accord each other they left him alone. He was allowed to grieve in his own way. As a boy who had just lost his mother he now had a special status.

Edward was fond of his three cousins, Florrie, Norah and Rita, who were a few years older. They liked Edward, boys being in short supply in the family. Ted had given Edward a series of large photographs taken by a friend of his who had visited Africa. Featured in the collection were a number of photos of handsome, naked black women. Edward had displayed these photos all over the walls of his bedroom.

Rita came to visit.

"Where's Edward?"

"He's gone to bed."

"I'll just creep up and see if he's still awake. If he's sleeping I won't disturb him."

It was a summer evening and not yet quite dark. Rita peeked into Edward's room and saw that he appeared to be asleep. Then she noticed the photographs and crept into the room to examine them more closely. In the dimness the dark figures had an eerie quality. She began to laugh. Edward woke up.

"What are you laughing at?"

"I like your taste, Edward."

Florrie and Rita married French Army officers whom they had met during the war. But before Rita moved to France at the end of the war to begin a new life with her husband, both her sisters were dead.

Soon after his return from the war three years later Ted married Constance, Kathleen's younger sister. Even though there was no blood relationship, censure arose when Ted married his sister-in-law. But gossip died away in face of Aunt

Constance's quiet dignity and obvious love for her nieces and nephew.

Aunt Constance was exquisite. She was petite with a tiny, round face, dancing brown eyes and a pert nose. Her long, black hair was wound round her head. There was laughter and life in the house again. In 1920, Bobby was born. Papa said,

" A boy. Good. He'll be able to work in the shop, too."

But Aunt Constance had other ideas and Bobby never did work in his father's shop. When he left school at the age of eighteen he began an apprenticeship with an engineering firm until he was called up in World War II.

In 1923, when baby Elizabeth was born, the older children idolized her. Elizabeth was flaxen-haired with tiny, perfect features and big, blue eyes. They danced attendance on her but she remained sweet-natured and unspoiled. Then at the age of two she fell ill with tuberculous meningitis. She became sicker and sicker; they held her little body as she was shaken with convulsions. And then the final stage of the dreadful disease was reached. She sank into a coma. The doctor had visited every day and came again one last time.

"There's nothing I can do. She won't last much longer."

Edward couldn't bear it. He couldn't bear to witness Aunt Constance's anguish. He went out and walked and walked and walked. When he came back, Aunt Constance was standing beside the body of her baby daughter, weeping silently. She would not leave Elizabeth's side. Eventually Katy led her gently away.

But tuberculosis had not finished with the family yet. A shadow which was to surface years later had been cast over Edward. And when she was only thirty-one Katy herself was to die from the disease.

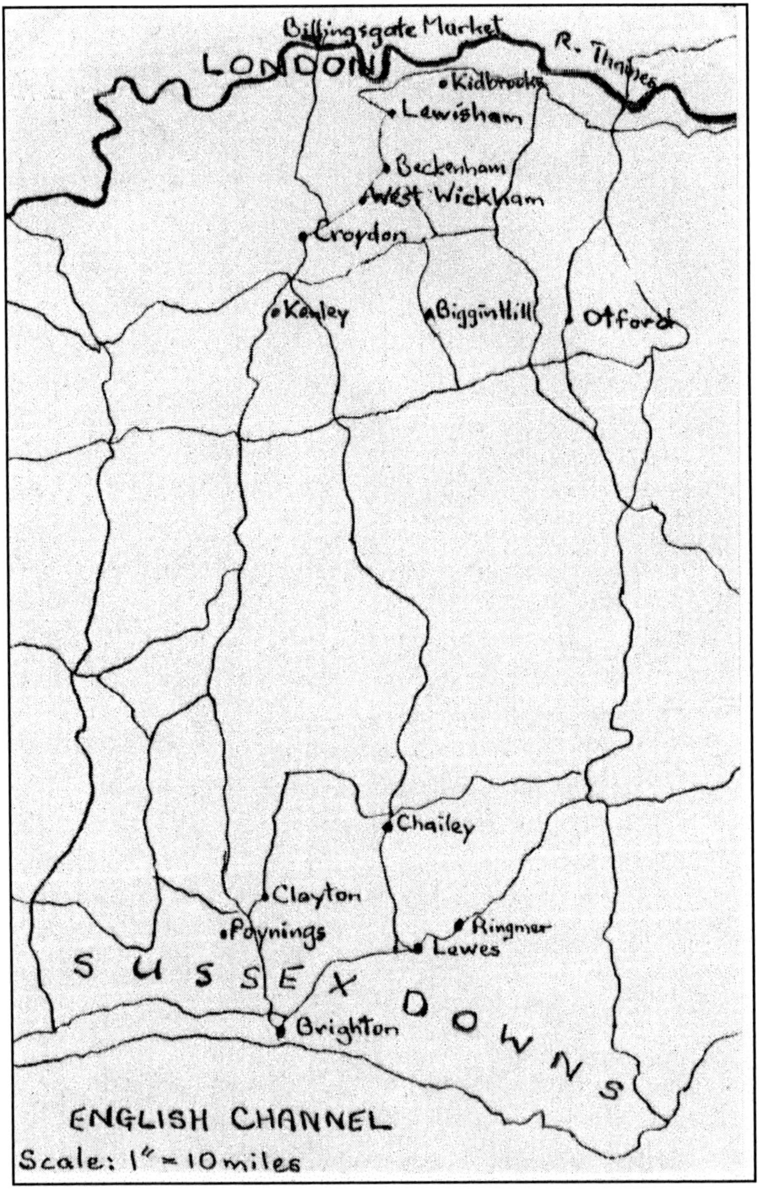
Billingsgate Market
LONDON
R. Thames
Kidbrooke
Lewisham
Beckenham
West Wickham
Croydon
Kenley
Biggin Hill
Otford
Chailey
Clayton
Poynings
Ringmer
Lewes
SUSSEX DOWNS
Brighton
ENGLISH CHANNEL
Scale: 1" = 10 miles

Printed by kind permission of The Sussex Archeological Society, from the Reeves' collection. Circa 1875

George Martin Coppard in front of his poulterer/fishmonger shop at 53 High Street, Lewes, with display of Christmas birds.

Four Generations of George Coppards

Standing: George Maynard
Seated: George Martin, George Herbert,
George Topley (baby)

THE GEORGES

After the war was won against Napoleon in 1815, prices of commodities in England fell suddenly. This ruined both farmers and businessmen and threw many people out of work. A controversial Corn Law, passed earlier that year, had been designed to help farming profits by preventing the importation of cheap grain. But in practice it did not work. Thousands of agricultural workers were starving.

George Coppard, Edward's great-great-grandfather, lived in Poynings, a little village five miles inland from the Sussex coast. Coppards are known to have lived in this area of Sussex since the fourteenth century. George and Sarah White from the nearby village of Clayton came to Brighton on the south coast of England in search of work. They were married in Brighton in 1818.

At this time, Brighton, fifty-nine miles from London, was growing faster than any other town in England. Doctors were advising their patients to bathe in the sea and the baths, drink waters from the sea, spring or spa and enjoy the healthy climate. When the Prince of Wales (later King George IV) and other wealthy people took up residence in the town, Brighton's popularity increased. To accommodate the visitors many fine houses were built.

Along with palatial residences, shops and hotels on the sea front, rows and rows of small buildings were erected in narrow back streets to house the servant population who served the visitors. They were cramped, airless, and unsanitary. Inferior materials were used in many of the houses. Some were so damp that lichen grew on the walls. The dwellings of the working classes in Brighton were even more overcrowded than those in towns of the industrial north. In these deplorable conditions contagious diseases such as consumption were rife.

George[1] and Sarah Coppard lived in one such slum, Darby Place, and began their married life together. Six of their nine children died of tuberculosis and other lung diseases. George was only forty-nine when he died and Sarah did not long survive him.

One of the three remaining children, George Coppard[2] left his life as a labourer in Brighton and in 1855 moved to Lewes, eight miles away, where he became a fishmonger/poulterer with his wife's family in Fisher Street. A few years later, he had his own business in High Street. In time, his son George Martin Coppard[3] took over the business, married, and continued the tradition of naming the oldest son George.

Victorian Lewes was a thriving county town, a flourishing centre of diverse commercial enterprises. The town also offered a wide range of activities: lectures, concerts, sports, circuses and fairs. Moreover, the seaside, at Brighton was only eight miles away.

High Street where the Coppards had their fish shop was the main avenue of commerce. There were over one hundred and forty shops and taverns, four hotels, the corn and hop exchange and various markets.

Seven children were born to George Martin and his wife:

---

[1] 1793-1841

[2] 1820-1897

[3] 1848-1924

George Maynard[4], Ted (Edward's father) Emily, Frank, Herbert (Bert), Robert (Bob) and Kathleen. The first five children were born in a room above the Coppard shop.

The brothers were good with their fists and were always sparring. They would scrap and fight and tease each other. The five boys slept in one room. One day Ted was complaining about his brothers' socks being so smelly, he couldn't stand it. Before bedtime that night his brothers smeared Gorgonzola cheese over the inside of his pillow-case. Ted came into the room.

"The stench in here is terrible. I can't sleep in this room!"

He took his pillow, Gorgonzola cheese and all, and went to sleep on the floor in the living room.

Ted's younger brother, Frank, was having trouble at school with a big bully called Buck who picked on him.

"Punch him once very hard on the nose," was George Martin's counsel.

The next day when Buck came after him again, Frank followed his father's advice and his tormentor, nose streaming blood, ran off howling. That night George Martin had already gone to bed when there was a prolonged banging on the front door. Irate at being woken when he had to get up very early the next morning to buy his fish, George leapt out of bed, strode to the window and threw it open. He looked down to see Buck's father standing there.

"What do you want?"

"Your son's broken my son's nose."

"Well, if I come down," said George, "I'm going to break your neck!"

He slammed down the window and went back to bed.

George Martin bought his fish every day in Brighton. A

[4] 1872-1937

tremendous variety was available. Oysters were dredged in the spring, mackerel caught in the summer, red mullet in May, lobsters and prawns in July. Herring and whiting were fished in the autumn along with plaice, sole, mullet, pilchards, dory, skate, turbot, sandrays and shrimp in season.

Then, before travelling back to Lewes to begin the day's selling, George Martin often took a swim around Brighton Pier.

At the back of the premises in High Street was the smokehouse where George Martin smoked haddock, his specialty.

George Martin was active in the life of the town, serving on a jury to choose two constables. He was also a great gambler and whiskey drinker. Some days he did not have the money to buy fish. He would send his oldest son, George Maynard, round the town hawking stale fish in a basket from door to door so that he could get enough money to buy fresh supplies.

After several years on his own at 53 High Street, George Martin joined forces with a partner, William Likeman. The shop flourished until the shipping company with whom they did a lot of business failed. In 1902, George Martin moved with his family to London and started a business in Billingsgate Market.

At the beginning of the new century Queen Victoria was dead after a reign of over sixty years. The British Empire covered one fifth of the globe and there was a population boom in Britain. The census showed that London was now a city of six and a half million people.

TED

My grandfather of the big, black beard was very proud of my father Ted. Ted was a sprinter. If he hadn't indulged too much in the beer when he wasn't training he'd probably have been very good.

Ted had the Coppards' deep chest and strong shoulders; he was of medium height but with longer legs than his father's. A good looking man with a strong, straight nose and piercing blue eyes, he wore a moustache and had a dimple in his chin.

As a young man, Ted was a fast sprinter. Each year Billingsgate Market had an Athletics Day, held at Stamford Bridge running track. One of many varied events was the porters' race where the porters ran a length of the track with boxes of fish balanced on their special hats.

One year Ted was the winner in the one hundred yards sprint at the Athletics Day. His father, George Martin, was very proud of his achievement and the next day, after a few drinks in *The Cock* public house, started boasting.

"Ted could break the record up the Monument you know."

"Nah, impossible."

"Bet he can," persisted George Martin. "He could do it in three minutes."

The Monument, about three hundred yards from the pub, had been built by Sir Christopher Wren to commemorate the fire of London in 1666. In the eighteenth century, tavern boys used to race up and down the steps of the two hundred foot column in two minutes thirty-two seconds. The building had continued to be a focus for the fishmongers to show off their athleticism and to make bets, although to the run they had added the distance from the pub to the monument and back.

Ted came into the bar and was told of his father's wager. Bets were laid. Stopwatches were pulled out. After suitable fortification, Ted stripped off his coat, took the proffered handkerchief from his father, and moved towards the door. Several customers walked outside and took up positions along the route.

"Ready?" asked Joe, standing at the door, stopwatch in hand.

He gave the signal and Ted was off, sprinting up the slight incline to the Monument, in through the door, and then up the steps, up each one of the three hundred and eleven separate steps, lungs bursting, legs on fire, to the top. Whatever had possessed his father to make such a boast? He'd never make it back down in time. A quick wave of his handkerchief for the benefit of those below; too bad he couldn't take a rest and enjoy the magnificent view. Then he was spilling down the spiral staircase and sprinting back to the Cock.

"He did it. He did it! Three minutes exactly!"

Ted was an intelligent, well-read man. In his last year at his public school in Lewes, Ted had been head boy. He enjoyed writing short stories. Following a meeting with a Russian émigré whom his daughter, Katy, brought home as a visitor, he took up the challenge to learn Russian. Katy was a member of the office staff of the Russian Government Committee in London and met several members of the Russian nobility who had fled to London in fear of the

Bolsheviks. At night school Ted learned the language very quickly and in 1918 he travelled to Archangel as an interpreter with the British Expeditionary Force under Field-Marshal Lord Ironside. On his return from Archangel Ted married Kathleen's sister, Aunt Constance.

Each morning when he left for Billingsgate Market, Ted was attired in pinstriped trousers, shirt, tie, jacket, high boots and bowler hat. As a Conservative member of the middle class it was important that he keep up appearances. When he came home at night, Bobby's job was to kneel in front of him as he sat in an armchair and take off his boots. Ted extended each foot in turn in front of him so that Bobby could undo the boot, pulling the lace through one grommet after another until the boot was loose enough to be pulled off. Bobby hated having to do this.

At the back of the house was a room known as the bicycle room. Ted bought himself a new bicycle with what was called a fairy cycle gear wheel. The gear was very small so that the rider had to pedal fast in order to move at any speed. Ted took Bobby by the neck, propelled him into the room, showed him the bike and said,

"Now look here. You see that bike? I don't want you ever to touch it. Got it?"

"Right, Papa."

Every morning, unless it was raining, Ted rode his bike to Penge East Station a mile or so away where he left it before taking the train to London. In the bicycle room he placed a clip around each of his trouser legs to prevent them from being caught in the gears, wheeled the bike outside, climbed aboard, adjusted his top hat, placed his furled umbrella under one arm and set off, legs pedalling furiously.

One rainy day Ted walked to the station. When he got home from school Bobby went into the bicycle room and stood admiring his father's bike. He flung open the outside door, leaped onto the bike and set off. The seat was too high, so he stood on the pedals. The rain had ceased and Bobby had a glorious time, cycling up one street and down another until he found himself at Penge East Station. He was out of breath and stood idly watching passengers emerge from the station. To his horror there was Papa. Bobby froze. Ted saw him, walked over, glowered at him and said,

"Give me those clips."

Bobby took the clips off the handlebars and handed them to his father. Papa bent down and put them on his trousers.

"Give me that bike."

He rode away and left Bobby standing at the station. When he got home, Ted said to Aunt Constance,

"Bobby was at the station with the bike. I was glad to see him. I'm tired and it saved me a walk. He'll be along soon."

Saturday nights Ted always came home with a great roast of meat from the market: beef or pork or lamb for Sunday dinner. Every Sunday Ted would go for a long walk with a neighbour, Mr. Cotton. Sunday dinner was served after Ted returned from his walk, sometimes not until late evening. When the meal was finished, the remainder of the roast would be left on the sideboard in the dining room for anyone to help themselves to whenever they wanted. It never lasted long.

Mr. Cotton was an avid walker.

"If you want to live to a good age, Mr. Cotton, you must walk, walk for your health," his doctor had advised.

So, rain or shine, he walked back and forth to the bank each day and with Ted every Sunday. They would leave after breakfast and walk for twenty-five or even thirty miles. Ted walked only on Sundays and the exertion just about killed him. But he rarely missed the challenge.

Like his father, Ted was a bully. His temper was unpredictable and the family took pains not to incur his wrath, especially when he had been drinking. He never hit his women folk but Edward was fair game. The blows came to an end, however, when Edward started boxing seriously. One evening when Papa went to hit him in his usual fashion Edward put up his fists. It was a reflex action acquired from his lessons in the boxing ring.

"You'd strike your father, would you?"

"No, Papa, I'd never strike you, but you won't hit me again, either. "

Edward used to spend time practising moves he learned in the boxing ring. One Sunday as the family waited for Papa to return from his walk, Edward was bouncing on his bed, shadow boxing. Bobby stood watching. Suddenly there was a terrific crash and the two end legs of the bed broke. Aunt Constance, Connie and Dorothy rushed upstairs to see what had happened. There was general consternation.

"What will your father say?" was Aunt Constance's concern.

"Get something to prop it up."

"The encyclopedias!" suggested Dorothy.

Ted had recently bought a set of encyclopedias which he had had bound in leather. Several volumes of the cherished books were hurriedly brought up to Edward's room, and while he and Dorothy lifted the end of the heavy bed, Connie placed the books underneath.

"Get the rest of the books, Bobby. We'll need them all."

Bobby staggered up the stairs with more volumes and they adjusted the books until the bed was level. Then the bedcover was draped to hide the makeshift repairs.

That evening a discussion began following an act of parliament ratified that week. Finally, in 1928, a law had been passed enabling women to vote at the age of twenty-one on an equal footing with men. Prior to that a woman had to be thirty before she could vote. Katy was angry.

"I'll be thirty-one before the next general election and I have a chance to vote. Women have been fighting for more than sixty years now, to get equality."

"Not as long as that, Katy," contradicted her father.

"Oh yes, indeed, Papa, more than sixty years, in fact."

Katy was never afraid to challenge her father.

"We'll settle the argument."

He pushed his chair back, got to his feet, and strode into the lounge to the bookcase. As he swept out there was silence. No one moved. There was a roar from the other room and he was soon back.

"Where are the encyclopedias?"

"In my room, Papa."

"Well, what are you sitting there for? Get the one we need, 'S' for suffrage!"

Edward left the room and took the stairs two at a time up to his bedroom. He flung back the bedcover, scanned the backs of the volumes, and with a Herculean effort lifted the bed with one hand as he pulled out the required book with the other.

"That took you long enough," said Papa, as Edward handed him the volume.

Next day with Papa safely at work, Edward's bed was repaired and the encyclopedias returned to their bookcase.

Troops on Parade

Field-Marshal Lord Ironside (centre) taking inspection in Aldershot, Kent, prior to the British Expeditionary Force to Archangel, Russia, 1918

Russian Government Committee and members of the Russian Aristocracy, London, 1918

Back row first left: Ted Coppard, interpreter and Russian correspondent
Front row first left: Katy Coppard, office staff member

FIRST DAY AT WORK

I listened to the carter's cries and heard the horses panting. I saw them straining and watched their great muscles moving up and down. Sparks flew off the cobbles from the horses' hoofs as they galloped over the bridge. I was fourteen and thought it was a wonderful sight.

Edward was fourteen and he had finished with school.

"You can have a few days to get yourself organized," said his father. "Aunt Constance will fit you out with clothes for work. You'll wear your good clothes to the market each morning and then change into a smock at the shop before beginning work."

Boys customarily wore short trousers until they were fourteen or fifteen. Now, Edward graduated to long ones. To denote his new status, Ted bought him a Trilby hat which he insisted Edward wear to and from work. Edward felt as if the world were sitting on his head. When he got home, the first thing he would do was to snatch the hat off his head and throw it in a corner.

It seemed like the middle of the night when Ted woke Edward at 4 a.m. for his first day at work. Feeling very self-conscious in his new attire: long grey trousers, white shirt, tweed jacket and hat, Edward accompanied Ted on the train journey from Penge East Station to London Bridge Station. Here they saw boxes of fish being unloaded from a train which had just arrived from the south coast of England. Each morning special fish trains ran from all the major fishing ports of Great Britain to the main London terminals in time for the fish to arrive at Billingsgate Market in London between 4 and 5 a.m.

"The boxes will be loaded onto carts and taken to Billingsgate. More fish is shipped by rail, now, than comes upriver to the dock. You'll see the names of the railway stations from which the fish is delivered on the sides of the carts," Ted told him. "Carts from the Great Central Railway, the North Western Railway, and others. They get as close to the market as they can. The streets they stop in around the market are known as the Inner Circle."

As they approached London Bridge, the cries of a carter sounded behind them. Edward looked back to see a big cart, drawn by two great drayhorses, loaded with boxes of fish on their way to Billingsgate Market. The carter, a huge older man, stood upright on the cart, whipping the horses into a gallop, and shouting to urge them on.

"They'd never make it up the slope unless he gets them into a gallop. Their hoofs can get no purchase on the cobbles."

Edward saw that there was a slight incline at the entrance to the bridge before it levelled off. The great animals passed them, their hoofs thundering on the cobbles. As Edward and his father walked over the bridge, several more carts, piled high with boxes, passed them. After they had crossed the river, they turned right onto Lower Thames Street and approached the market.

Edward could not believe his eyes. It seemed there were horses; horses; horses and carts everywhere. Long lines of horses and carts stood one behind the other, four deep, outside the market. On any given day, a thousand tons of fish might be brought into Billingsgate Market within the space of a few hours.

But Ted was leading the way to the opposite side of the

street where *The Cock*, 'the fishmongers' pub' was located. *The Cock* had a special license to be open from 5 a.m. to 9 a.m. To the side of the bar on the right was a big blackboard showing all the arrivals of fish into Billingsgate from Scotland, Ireland, the West and East coasts; from all over the British Isles. The pub was filled with buyers, getting the latest information on fish catches before they made their purchases in the market.

"You see the board here, Edward, I have to make decisions as to what and when to buy. If there's another big arrival of a particular fish then the price might go down within the hour. The information on the board is like a horse-racing tip."

Edward watched while a man wrote on the board:

HULL 50 TONS COD

"Now we'll go into the market, you'll see your grandfather's stand, and then I'll make my purchases. For a few days you can just watch what goes on. You'll get the hang of it soon enough."

They left the pub and began to cross the street towards the market, weaving their way between the carts. Edward ducked under the head of a huge horse only to feel it lunge down, ready to bite.

"You need to watch out if you do that," warned Ted, "unless you want to get nipped."

A steady stream of porters, in their long white coats, came to the carts, taking the boxes of fish into the market to one of more than two hundred stands from which fish was sold. Other porters carried fish in from the wharfage alongside the market where laden boats arrived each morning.

One of the rules of the porters' union was that every packet of fish sold at Billingsgate Market had to be carried in on a porter's head and pitched onto a stand.

A porter wore a special leather hat with a flat top, custom-made to fit the shape of his head, on which he would carry as much as ten stone (140 pounds). The hat had an upturned rim designed to catch any run-off from the boxes. The hats were called bobbin hats, similar to the helmets worn by the British archers at Agincourt.

But before he invested in the considerable expense of such a hat, he would become one of a 'string', a kind of union. He wore a white smock to which was pinned an enamel licence badge denoting his trade. He could earn very good money. Without the porters, Billingsgate Market could not have functioned effectively.

Ted and Edward made their way to the stand owned by Ted's father, George Martin. Each of the stands in the market specialized in a particular kind of fish. George Martin's speciality was haddock.

"What do you think, Edward," asked his grandfather, "do you think you're going to like the scene here?"

"Is it always as busy as this?"

"Wait 'til Friday if you want to know what busy is. Everyone wants fish on Fridays. I've told your father to have you spend a day with me. I'll show you around and tell you a thing or two."

In the sixteenth century Queen Elizabeth I had decreed both Wednesdays and Fridays to be meatless days. This was done not because of religious beliefs but in the interests of keeping British seamen and ships busy. In more recent times the extra consumption of fish was confined to Fridays. Moreover, many people, not just Catholics, chose to eat fish on Fridays.

While George Martin and Ted were talking, Edward watched what was going on. By this time, 7 a.m., the market was in full spate. Hundreds of retail buyers from all over London and a wide area beyond were converging on the market: fishmongers, fish fryers, restauranteurs, hoteliers, and costermongers. The largest single group of buyers were the costermongers who sold their fish from barrows on the streets throughout London. The carts to which buyers' purchases were taken had to be parked in streets further away from the market, within a radius of about half a mile, known as the Outer Circle. By 9 a.m. most of the buying would be done because the surrounding streets had to be cleared for regular traffic.

Inside the cavernous building there was a tremendous amount of noise and movement as buyers converged on the market but it was not chaotic; rather, it was apparent that everyone knew exactly where they were going and why. On the floor an increasing amount of icy slush and fish slime collected, dripped from the boxes. There was a pronounced fishy smell everywhere, penetrating and clinging.

Edward watched the porters going back and forth in their long white coats, piles of boxes balanced on their heads. On their necks, the muscles stood out like whipcords. He noticed how people took care to keep out of the path of the porters, not wishing to be sworn at. Their predecessors, the fishwives of earlier days, had also carried fish on their heads, in baskets or buckets. The fishwives' behaviour had given rise to the word 'billingsgate', meaning: abuse, violent invective. Indeed, 'fishwife' can be used to describe a vulgar, abusive woman.

"Come, Edward, we're off to get today's prices. One of the things I'll want you to do each morning is to note the difference in price from one stand to another. Today, remember how much each stand is asking for cod. You'll notice the huge variety of fish available, but I don't carry more than a dozen or so on any one day."

As they looked at the stands, Edward noted that prices might differ by a few pence. P.W. Larkin's cod was two shillings and sixpence a stone whereas J.A. Bacon's was three shillings a stone. When Ted had got the information he needed, he said,

"Right, now I'll buy."

He moved from stand to stand, buying for the best prices; plaice, with their distinctive red spots, haddock, cod, iridescent herring, turbot with their light brown backs, dappled mackerel, and more.

"Look at these," said Ted, stopping in front of another stand. "These are Norwegian salmon, ten to fifteen pounds each. They're rich. When they come in, the oil's running out of the bottom of the boxes. We get lots of salmon from Ireland and Scotland. The Scotch salmon commands a good price."

Turbot! Turbot! All alive turbot! shouted a salesman, standing atop his table and roaring out his price.

Ha-a-ansome cod! Best in the market! All alive! Alive Oh!

As Ted made his purchases, the boxes were placed on the head of the porter who'd been engaged to carry them to a costermonger's barrow outside the market. Then Edward and his father walked behind the costermonger as he strained between the shafts, pulling the barrow to Draper Street a mile away where Ted had his shop.

Lower Thames Street

Scene outside Billingsgate Market to left, Cock Public House on right, looking up Monument Street to The Monument

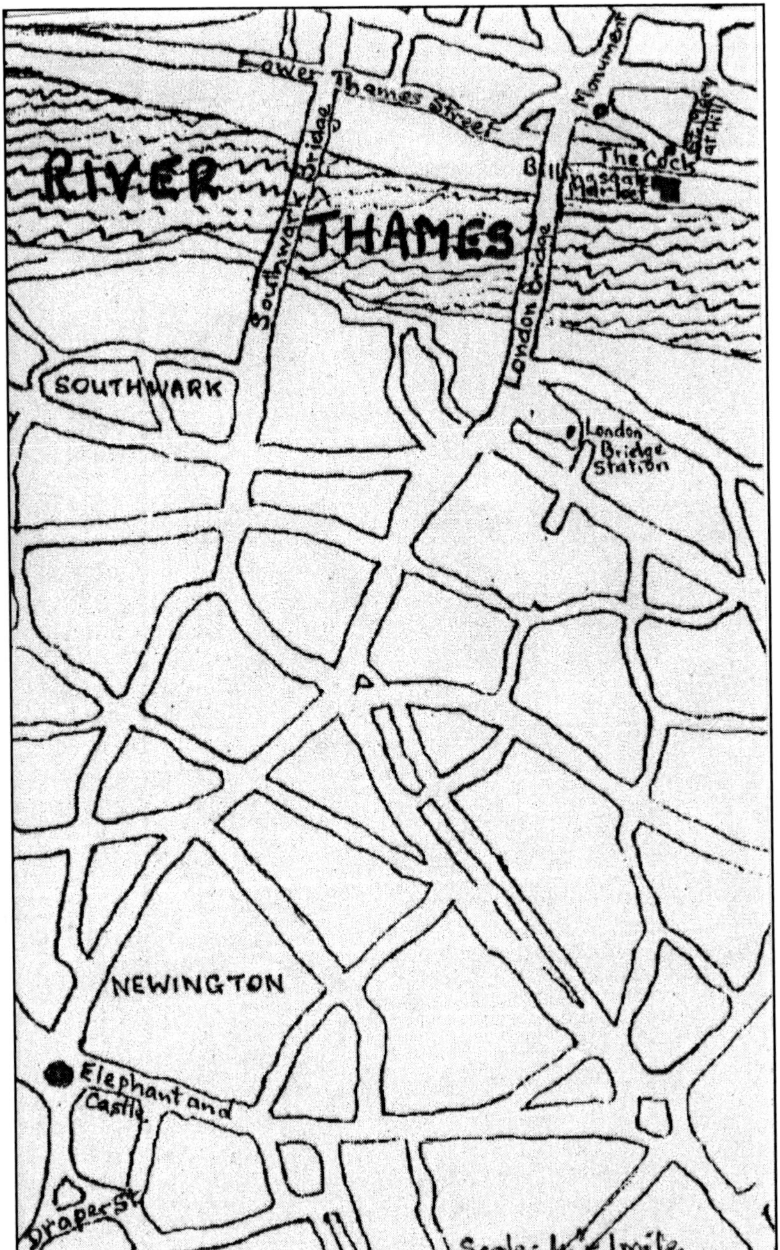
Lower Thames Street
Monument
Fish St Hill
The Cock
Billingsgate Market
RIVER
THAMES
Southwark Bridge
London Bridge
SOUTHWARK
London Bridge Station
NEWINGTON
Elephant and Castle
Draper St
Scale: ¼" = 1 mile

BILLINGSGATE MARKET

Inside the market each morning it was organized chaos with everyone frantically buying and selling. But outside it was complete pandemonium. I used to watch the porters, boxes balanced on their heads, as they wove their way through the snarled-up traffic. I loved the clamour and the crowds. And then, miraculously, by 9 a.m., the hubbub had ceased and the vehicles were all gone.

The Cock had been built in 1889 on the site of an earlier building of the same name. It was a very informal pub patronized by all the market people. Boxes of fish were quite likely to be dropped on the seats by the porters while they had their beer, and by the end of the day a patron might find himself kicking around a few fishheads amongst the other debris on the floor.

Each morning it took Edward about twenty minutes to go round the stands in the market and price the fish his father wanted to buy. Keeping the figures in his head - he never had to write the numbers down - he would return with the information to the pub.

"Could you use a hot toddy, boy?" Ted asked him.

Edward nodded and as he was underage, Ted fetched it for him. Edward would sip the rum and hot milk slowly, feeling fire burn his belly, then the tingling in his toes and fingers. On a cold winter's morning this was everyone's favourite beverage.

Billingsgate has been associated with the sale of fish for

more than one thousand years. It was initially a small port which handled general cargo. The neighbouring port of Queenhythe, up river from London Bridge, was originally more favoured because of royal patronage. King Henry III, in 1227, ordered all fish landed elsewhere to be seized.

An Act of Parliament, in 1699, made Billingsgate a free and open market for all kinds of fish with the exception of eels. The sale of eels was restricted in favour of Dutch fishermen because of their help in feeding Londoners during the Great Fire. Billingsgate soon outstripped its rival Queenhythe and became the biggest inland wholesale fish market in the world.

Billingsgate was renowned for speed and dependability. There was always a tremendous variety of fresh fish available. Fish sold at Billingsgate was always of good quality. A team of inspectors regularly examined fish to ensure its freshness. Under the market were huge cold-storage facilities, known as the lazaret, where at the end of the day, any unsold fish was stored.

As Edward became familiar with the way the market worked, he gained increasing respect for the porters. They were the cream of the musclemen of London. But their working life was short. Injuries and deaths were not infrequent. Harry, an immensely powerful man, was proud of his strength and used to carry more boxes of fish on his head than any other man, sometimes as much as twenty stone. One day as he was pulling a huge load of boxes on a cart, he collapsed between the shafts, and died. Several men died in this way.

Opposite the market, on the corner of Monument Street and St. Mary-at-Hill was a Christian Mission. Medical treatment for minor injuries was provided for all the local workers.

Billingsgate Market was situated at the level of the river, and the streets leading away from it were all uphill. The steep inclines presented a problem for the porters. At the foot of St. Mary-at-Hill and Dunstan's Hill, the barrows, piled high with boxes, would all be waiting to be moved. When the load on a barrow was complete, the porter would go round to where homeless men had spent the night, sleeping in doorways.

He'd call out, "Up the hill! Up the hill!"

Emerging from wherever they had managed to find shelter, several vagrants would appear, anxious to earn a few pence. When three or four men had come forth, the porter got between the shafts of the cart and pulled, while the men pushed from behind. When they got to the top of the hill he could well afford to pay them sixpence or a shilling from the twenty to thirty pounds a week he earned. One of the longest runs a porter made was from the market to Tower Bridge yard near Traitors' Gate.

When the last of the carts had been moved, the porters went to one of several pubs in the area which had special licenses to remain open. Here they stayed, available for work if needed. Sometimes the porters' days extended from five in the morning to nine at night.

One day after he had done the pricing of the fish for his father as usual, Edward spent the rest of the day with his grandfather. George Martin did not come to the market every day, however. He was in his seventies by the time Edward first started work. George Martin's sons had taken over the stand, one of over two hundred in the market, and owned various retail businesses in the area where he had helped them to get established.

Edward looked at the figure of his grandfather with his

bald pate atop a big black beard. He seemed as powerful as ever. George Martin's clear, resonant voice could be heard all over the market. He introduced Edward to the owner of the stand next to him.

"So this is Ted's son, eh? That Ted was a card in his younger days. What about the time he took off for a fight with the Jewish boy and left your stand with no one here?"

"I never knew that," said Edward.

"Oh, yes. Your grandfather here left him in charge one day when along came Simon. He'd won a match the night before at Premierland where the Jewish boys box and we were all congratulating him.

Then Ted says, 'You think you're so good. Maybe I could beat you.'

'Right,' says Simon, 'come on down then.'

So they went down to the lazaret because no one's allowed to fight in the market here. They started fighting. Ted had the upper hand for a while and then suddenly Simon put on the pressure, and knocked Ted out cold.

When your grandfather came back, he yelled,

'Where's Ted?'

I told him he was down in the lazaret, fighting Simon for a two shilling bet.

'Good God,' shouted George Martin, 'there's no one here now. The other boys are off in the army fighting the Germans and Ted's down below, fighting a Jewish boy to win a bet.'"

From time to time there were special events held in the Market.

"You'll be able to see the fish filleting competition today," George Martin told Edward. "It's quite a spectacle, but first I'll take you to my favourite coffee shop."

They left the bustling activity and noise of the market to

be confronted outside by a tremendous traffic jam. The streets were packed solid. Weaving their way through the mass of vehicles, Edward and his grandfather headed up St. Mary-at-Hill. As they walked by the church, George Martin said,

"Every October we have a harvest festival here. You'll see the church decked out with boats and nets and different kinds of fish."

When they got to the café, one of several in the street, Edward followed his grandfather as he elbowed his way through the throng. 'Fish' people of all sorts crowded the cafe amidst a clamour of voices. The aroma of the market was very much in evidence.

George Martin boomed the order.

"We'll have two bowls of oysters, and hot bread and coffee."

There seemed to be no room to sit anywhere but when George Martin's friends saw him they made space at their table for him and Edward. George Martin introduced Edward.

"This here's my grandson, Ted's boy. He's learning the business."

Two heaping bowls of oysters were placed in front of them. George Martin turned to Edward,

"I'll be talking to my friends here. Take your time, boy, we're not in any hurry."

The preliminaries of the filleting competition were over by the time Edward and George Martin came back to the market. One of the finalists stood at his table, bare-armed, in his striped apron, waiting for the signal to begin. On the floor at the end of the table was a box into which would fall the pieces he discarded. To the side of his table were six different fish. He would have twenty minutes to dress them in six different ways: skin and curl a whiting; wing and skin a whole skate; fillet a flounder; steak a cod; skin and trim a lemon sole; bone a herring.

'How can he do all that in twenty minutes?' wondered Edward. The bell sounded; the contestant's fingers flew and the knife flashed as he dissected the fish.

"I can bone a herring but not nearly as fast as he can."

"You will, you will," reassured George Martin. "Give yourself time."

By six o'clock, after Edward had left to go home, the market was silent and still, the streets outside bare, the throngs dispersed; no horses, no carts, no people.

DRAPER STREET

The Cockneys were warm-hearted and full of life, with quick repartee. They joked and bantered with each other and with their customers. I admired their self- deprecating, dry sense of humour.

In 1920, George Martin bought Ted a fish shop in Draper Street. Draper Street, in South London, was short, flanked on one end by Newington Butts and on the other by Walworth Road. On the north side were the Drapers' Almshouses (Rowton House) and five shops: a corn dealer, a tobacconist, a wardrobe maker, a hairdresser and a hostler. On the south side were a fried fish shop, a dairy, an eel-pie house, a marine store, a coffee shop, a costumier, a linen-draper, a haberdasher, a confectioner, a chandler, a china and glass dealer and Ted's shop, number 4. Over the door was the inscription:

EDWARD T. COPPARD
FISHMONGER AND CURER

In front of his shop Ted set up a stall each morning from where he sold cheaper cuts of fish. At the back of his premises was the smokehouse where he cured haddock. This was his speciality and was very popular.

On his bags was printed:

COPPARD'S HOME-CURED HADDOCK

Ted supplied fish to the Almshouses and to various hotels and businesses. The shop was always busy, selling an immense selection of fish, and did well financially.

In addition to the variety of shops, there were stalls set up each day on the south side of Draper Street. Each shopkeeper was entitled to put a stall in front of his shop but not all of them used their space. The regulations were that stalls had to be set out by 8:30 a.m. or the spot could be used by someone else. A citizen of London had the centuries-old right to erect a stall and trade in the allotted street-market pitches but he often needed to beat someone else to it. Space was at a premium and there were frequent fights to secure a pitch.

Twice a week Edward delivered fish to the Almshouses across the street. He walked through the door in the high wall behind which some of the old men would sit on a sunny day. They always spoke to him, enjoying the contact with a young person.

" 'Ow's the luv life, Edward?"

"We 'eard you done good in the ring last night."

Ted supplied eels to the eel-pie shop where he and Edward were frequent customers. In addition to pies, the shopkeeper served bowls of eels. The eels were cooked in a parsley soup and on a cold winter's night a dish of eels with hot, crusty rolls made a wonderful meal.

Eels, eels, all jelly,
Make you fat and fill your belly

Cries were called out continuously by vendors:

Fish makes brains and bonny babies
Meat drives you potty

Another popular dish was a plate of mussels. Mussels grew in profusion around the English coast, were gathered into big sacks, brought to London and sold cheaply.

Herring made a cheap, nutritious meal. As the shoals of herring travelled round the coast from the north-east of Scotland, southwards to the English Channel and on into the Irish Sea, Scottish girls followed to where the catches were landed, and processed the fish. A percentage of the herring was split and smoked to make kippers. Ted sold a lot of kippers.

Unprocessed herring was also very popular. The soft roe was much in demand. Served on toast with anchovy sauce, it was considered a delicacy. Everyone wanted soft rather than hard roes.

Full-roed 'erring, full-roed,
Soft one side and 'ard the uver.

Edward played up to the customers, enjoying the banter with which a sale was conducted.

"Can I 'ave a cupla pounds of soft-roed 'errin'?"

"Well awright, ducks, I'll give 'em to you as a great favour. I shouldn't pick 'em all out soft for you, although you are a lovely lady."

The patter varied with each customer.

"Want me to pick you out six soft-roed herring? Alright, tell you what, I'll give you four soft and two hard. Can't give you all the softs now, can I?"

The transaction completed, he'd sing out,

"Sold! Sold to the lady wiv all 'er clo'es on."

The shopkeeper next door to Ted never used his stall space and every day without fail Gerry, a big, jovial costermonger, popular with customers, beat the competition and set up his stall in front of the shop. When Ted or Edward arrived to open their premises, Gerry's stall was always in place, ready for the day's vending.

"I think Gerry must camp here overnight," said Edward.

"He lives just round the corner; gets here about six each morning."

There was a great variety of fresh produce in the market and Edward looked forward to the arrival of strawberries from the fields in Kent each June. He loved cycling through Kentish lanes on a beautiful Sunday morning, especially after a light rain, smelling the heady, sweet aroma from the strawberry fields on either side.

Mornin' gavered strawberries,
Mornin' gavered.

The musical patter of calls from stallholders was continuous. The market pulsed with people, sounds and smells.

Ol' ladies' pears,
Ol' ladies' pears,

referred to big Williams' pears, soft to eat, easy for old women with no teeth because of lack of dental treatment.

Some calls reflected the Cockney's cleverness with words, his love of a play on words:

Sprats like water
Muvver likes gin (sotto voce)

(Sprats, tiny fish, fall like water as they cascade through the fishmonger's fingers.)

Back slang was used by traders so that customers were not

able to understand what they were saying. Edward could check with Ted as to what price he was charging for a particular fish.

"Ecrip of eslaps?" (what's the price of plaice?)

"Ena the dunna" (nine pence a pound)

Irish Cockneys, as they were sometimes called, descendants of those who had fled Ireland in the famine years of the 1840s, shopped in the market. The women had no shopping baskets but would gather up their aprons in front of them to make a receptacle for their purchases.

Mondays were quiet in the market, and Mary, a gypsy fortune teller, came around reading palms. She was tall and swarthy, with long colourful skirts and a bright bandana on her head. For sixpence she would read your palm. Sometimes, if she had a good day, she gave the old ladies a special deal for a penny. A hustler accompanied her.

"Now, give them all a good reading, Madam, give them all a good reading."

"Come and have your fortune told. You never know what life holds for you."

After having her palm read, an old lady would return to her friends in great excitement,

"Yer know what she told fer me?"

Edward liked and admired the Cockneys who worked in the market. They never had any money but could always laugh, frequently at themselves. No matter how hard their lives, they never indulged in self-pity. They were generous and would always help someone in trouble. They expected little but knew an immense enjoyment of life.

People were tough. If they were sick, they went to work just the same. Edward had an impacted wisdom tooth, and after several days of severe pain, went one morning to a dentist.

"This is going to be painful. You need a bit of common-or-garden British pluck."

After giving him a painkiller, the dentist extracted the tooth. Edward went out into a cold, biting wind, walked back to his father's shop and started working.

"How did you get on?"

Without waiting for an answer, Ted turned his attention to a customer who had just come up. As the sedative wore off, Edward's jaw gave him excruciating pain, but he continued working to the end of the day.

As they stood on the train station on their way home, Ted asked,

"You'll be able to make it in the morning, won't you?"

Even though by the next day Edward's jaw was dreadfully inflamed and still very painful, he went to market as usual. He would not have dreamed of telling Ted he was in too much pain to come to work.

Jimmy was a little Cockney man who worked in Draper Street. His nose was completely flat, it had no bridge and hair grew out of it. He was a very ugly small man but his bright, beady eyes were always full of life and good humour. He was well liked.

"What happened to Jimmy?"

"They say his mother dropped him when he was a baby," said Ted, "she was drunk."

Jimmy had no regular job but was always in demand by the costermongers, who paid him a shilling or half a crown to pack apples, run errands or sweep up. He was always at hand when a cargo of goods needed unloading.

Beer used to be delivered to customers on great drays pulled by a couple of horses. On his way to a pub with a load one day, a drayman left his horses unattended while he went across the street for an eel pie. There was a huge crash as a load of boxes tipped over, and the massive drayhorses, each about eighteen hands high, took fright and bolted.

Jimmy suddenly appeared, grabbed hold of the reins of one horse and hung on for dear life as the horses careened down Draper Street, knocking everything aside as they went. Barrels of beer fell off the dray and rolled into stalls, toppling them over. Jimmy was swung and knocked about but managed to bring the horses to a stop. As the driver came running up, Jimmy said,

"You betta watch them 'orses, mate, someone's gonna get killed." He limped off.

A few weeks later a deputation comprising the mayor, a police superintendent and three other officials proceeded down Draper Street. They asked for Jimmy. Everyone immediately sprang to Jimmy's defense. If a policeman was in evidence it usually meant someone was about to be arrested.

"What d'you want 'im for, po'r little bugger?"

" 'e ain't done nofink."

"No, it's not like that at all. We have something to give him. We want to speak to Jimmy."

By this time a crowd had gathered, wondering what on earth the mayor might have to say to Jimmy. Jimmy was eventually produced. Cap on head, he made his way through the crowd towards the mayor.

"What d'you want, guv?" asked Jimmy, as he doffed his cap.

The mayor spoke.

"We heard that at considerable risk to yourself you brought a team of runaway horses under control. You could have been killed. It's likely you prevented other people from being killed or injured. We would like to honour your bravery by making you a presentation. What better place to do it than in Draper Street."

The mayor handed Jimmy a gold watch and ten gold sovereigns. Jimmy was speechless until everyone began cheering.

"Fanks, guv, fanks," and he disappeared into the crowd.

At night, tanks of paraffin were brought in from which flares were lit. A big flame was thrown out, providing a good light for the costermongers' stalls. Sometimes fires were started when someone placed boxes or debris too near the flares.

Above Ted's shop was a room where he and Edward changed their clothes before going home. From the street below, teeming with people, Edward could hear the sounds of costermongers' cries and the hubbub of the market. There was no electricity, only the eerie light from a myriad flares flickering on the walls and dancing on the ceiling.

Dorothy Coppard circa 1930

ELEPHANT AND CASTLE

The Elephant and Castle vibrated with life night and day. It was always crowded but I loved the people. It was dirty, it was noisy and it was wonderfully alive.

The Elephant and Castle, in South London, at the confluence of six streets, was once known as the *Piccadilly of the South* (London). The district took its name from the leading pub in the area.

One of the more unlikely explanations for the name itself is that it is a corruption of *L'Enfanta de Castille*, the name given to the pub in the reign of Charles I when he was briefly engaged to the Crown Princess of Spain. The fact that neither word is to be found in the Spanish language itself, however, does not seem to detract from the romanticism of the explanation.

The Trocadero, at the Elephant and Castle, was one of several vast super-cinema theatres which were built between the wars. They had enormous electric organs, Wurlitzers, and big stages on which shows were mounted to entertain patrons between feature films.

The Rockingham, a huge pub in the neighbourhood, had the longest bar in the city, or so it was claimed. The brewery which owned the pub always engaged publicans of great girth, tall, good-looking and jovial. Mr. and Mrs. Andover, in their mid-forties, certainly fitted these criteria. They were both of a height, almost six feet; she was a big-bosomed, handsome woman and he was strong and muscular. They were popular with the customers and there was seldom any trouble in *The Rockingham* when they were behind the bar.

The main attraction of the pub was the long bar where all the women, the 'talent', sat. They had to be over the age of eighteen. About twenty feet away was a circular bar where the men stood drinking, eyeing the girls. If a man fancied a particular girl, he would gesture to her and she would get up and come towards him.

"How much, dear? Just remember I only want to borrow it for a while, not buy it."

Sometimes only a brief stand-up contact, a 'knee-trembler,' would be made, the girl charging five shillings. If the client wanted an hour of her time or maybe all night, the price varied from seven to twelve shillings. The girl would lead the man back to her tenement room in a street so narrow that you could almost shake hands with a person on the other side. Gonorrhea was rife and also the more serious venereal disease, syphilis, but treatment could be had at any hospital for a small fee.

There was also a private bar in the pub - jug and bottle as it was called - where take-away alcohol was available. An old lady could creep in with a jug tucked under her black shawl and get beer or gin without her husband knowing.

When he was seventeen, Edward was introduced to the scene at *The Rockingham.*

"Come wiv us tonight, Edward," said John, a costermonger Edward knew. "Maybe yer'll see someone yer fancy."

In the evening, Edward and John made their way to *The Rockingham* and joined the crowd of men at the bar. They ordered their beers and surveyed the situation. There were a dozen or so women seated across the room and Edward witnessed several transactions. As he looked across at the women he noticed a girl who did not look as if she could possibly be eighteen. Her hair was a flaming red and under the light her skin appeared translucent. She was beautiful. After observing her for a while it seemed to Edward that she was making no effort to have eye contact with any man. He wondered who she was.

"See anyone yer might like?"

Edward shook his head.

"I'm on me way then," said John, as he moved to meet a woman who was coming towards him. "See yer termorrer."

The girl was still sitting against the wall as Edward finished his next beer. He didn't want to think about her going off with any man. Then he questioned Mrs. Andover.

"She's Irish. Her name's Meghan. It's the usual story; a new immigrant, she was raped and now her family will have nothing to do with her. Her brother beat her up when he found out. She'll never be able to marry one of her own. She feels that this is all she's good for."

Edward felt a great compassion for Meghan but there was nothing he could do to help her. He didn't go to *The Rockingham* again.

Betty Neville, a customer of Edward's, lived at the Elephant and Castle. Betty, a small, wiry woman with black hair and bright blue eyes, did her best for her family. There were eight of them. Her husband, Bob, an easy-going fellow, was a labourer and never steadily employed. They shared a house with six other people. Betty's family had three rooms unless Bob was out of work for more than a month. Then, in order to avoid eviction for non-payment of rent, one room would be sublet and they would all crowd into the two remaining rooms.

Poor as they were, Betty and her fellow tenants 'kept up appearances'. The women took turns scrubbing the stairs and cleaning the one outside toilet shared by them all. They might have cardboard to cover the holes in the soles of their shoes, but the uppers were clean and polished. It was a matter of pride.

The nearest to a holiday many Cockneys had was each September when they departed en masse for the hop fields in Kent. Special trains were run from London Bridge Railway Station. Betty Neville took her whole family each year. She got everything organized with all they would need for two or three weeks and then they set off.

Bob Neville walked in front carrying a huge bundle of bedding tied up with string. Behind him came the children, all six of them, each carrying something. Bringing up the rear was Mrs. Neville, wheeling the old pram which had been got out of pawn for the occasion, stacked high with pots and pans and clothes.

On their way to London Bridge they promenaded through Draper Street, calling 'goodbyes' to everyone as if they were leaving for a year or more.

" 'ave a luverly time then, Betty."

"You nippers pull yer weight now, eh?"

"Don't drink it all up then, Bob."

The procession stopped at Ted's shop.

"What'll you have, Betty?" Edward asked.

"I'll 'ave two poun' o' smoked 'addock, please. It won't go orff afore termorrer."

"Here's some roes for tonight," and Edward handed her an extra package. "They're ready cooked for you."

"Ta, love, we'll enjoy those."

She bought eight apples from Gerry's stall and stuffed her purchases down the sides of the pram next to her bottle of gin.

" 'ere's some fer the train," said Gerry, and gave each of the children another apple.

The train took them from London Bridge to Maidstone, in Kent, from where a truck transferred them to a farm on the River Medway. When they arrived at the farm they laid claim to a hut in which to sleep and got themselves sorted out. Then they feasted on the roes between slices of bread. When they were hopping, Betty cooked only one hot meal a day, before they started the day's work.

Next morning, after a breakfast of smoked haddock, they were in the fields by seven where the whole family picked hops until five o'clock in the afternoon. The basket into which they threw the hops was almost as high as the smallest Neville child. With all of the family working they managed to pick forty bushels. It was hard work and by the end of the day everyone's fingers were sore and black from the hops.

In the evenings Bob departed for the local pub where the hoppers were allowed on sufferance. Many of the pubs had signs in the windows stating that hoppers and gypsies would not be served. The children made for the river where they devised their own games. Betty sat outside the hut talking with the other women and indulging in a little drop of comfort from time to time. For the women it was a welcome respite from the unrelenting drudgery of their lives at home in the slums of London.

At the end of three weeks, on their way back from London Bridge Station, they paraded triumphantly through Draper Street Market, the children showing off their sunburnt noses, and with arms full of wild flowers picked in the woods. Bob strutted at the head of the line, jangling the few shillings he had left in his pockets.

" 'ow're yer goin', Bob? Got any bees and 'oney (money) left?"

"You kids 'ad a good time, eh?"

" Good to see yer, Betty. 'ow was it then?"

"I got drunk on the fresh air. Luverly it was, luverly."

Edward Coppard circa 1927

DANCING AND PARTIES

We had a huge house with lots of space and Katy and Connie used to put on some wonderful big do's. People would come to our house and we'd have a drink and then go across the road to play tennis. We had a coterie of young people and we quite fancied ourselves.

After Aunt Constance's baby Elizabeth died, Ted and his family left Avenue Road, moving a few times before finally settling in Croydon Road. They had a huge, four-storied house, with a big bay window each side of the front door. To the right of the door was the sitting room at the end of which was a large table where the family sat for meals on Sundays and when people were entertained. To the left of the front door was the lounge where the young people had parties and danced. Shelves lined the walls of this room holding Ted's extensive collection of books. Both rooms were enormous, stretching along the depth of the house.

From the central hallway, stairs led down to the kitchen where the family ate most of their meals. When meals were eaten in the dining room, everything had to be carried back and forth. The butler's room beyond the kitchen became the bicycle room. Another room was big enough to hold a ping-pong table. Upstairs were four large bedrooms, and, as usual for that time, only one bathroom. Attic rooms above the bedrooms provided playing space for Bobby and his friends.

Across the road were the premises where the Conservative Club, to which Ted belonged, held meetings and socials. More in keeping with the interests of Edward, Katy, Connie and Dorothy was the house adjacent to it with grounds big enough for a tennis court where they were often invited to play.

Aunt Constance was engrossed with her young son, Bobby, and if Ted was at home, he was often drinking, and didn't concern himself with his older children's activities. The house hummed with young people constantly coming and going, and Katy used any excuse to have a group of friends over or to throw a party.

The Avenue Road house had not been big enough for a large party. In any event Katy's twenty-first birthday, in 1919, had passed uncelebrated because of the influenza epidemic which was raging. In 1918 and 1919, the Spanish flu, as it was called, killed more people than did the war. In one week alone, in October of 1918, more than two thousand people died in London. Day after day funeral cortèges passed down the street.

"Fred Bingham, the man they gave the white feather to, is dead. So his mother didn't save him after all," said Ted.

When Connie came of age in 1924, they had had a small party for her. But for Edward's birthday in 1926, with a big house at her disposal, Katy organized a splendid party in his honour. Edward was shy and embarrassed at being the centre of attention.

"You'll enjoy it," Katy assured him.

She invited everyone they knew. The girls came with hair bobbed or shingled, in dresses of the latest style. The silhouette was tubular, with flattened busts and lowered waists. Hemlines were daringly raised to the calf. The few men Katy was able to round up for the party wore double-breasted suits.

Dorothy brought her friend, Adèle, the daughter of a French Army officer killed in the war. In contrast to the older girls, her long black hair cascaded down her back. She had a pert little nose, sparkling black eyes, a provocative smile, and Edward found her French accent captivating. At twenty-one he fell madly in love.

The gramophone cabinet, an elegant piece of furniture on long legs, took pride of place in the lounge. On the night of the party, everyone brought their favourite jazz and dance records and the gramophone played all night, the needle hissing as it moved through the grooves. A willing arm was always available to change the needle and wind up the gramophone at the end of each number.

Throughout the twenties, there was a craze for dancing. The favourites were the foxtrot, one-step and the waltz. The Black Bottom, an ugly footstomping dance, made a brief appearance and other new dances - the Jog Trot, the Vampire, and the Shimmy - came and went. The Charleston, imported from the United States, required unaccustomed movements, knees moving together and apart, and then as the partners separated, wild kicking out of the feet. It was greeted with outrage.

"It is neurotic! It is rotten! It stinks!" was one clergyman's pronouncement.

Even the press viewed it as degenerate. It was thought that one's ankles would become permanently deformed. Then the Prince of Wales learned how to do the dance and suddenly the Charleston become acceptable and everyone learned it. One dance instructor, Santos Casani, demonstrated the Charleston from the top of a taxi as it was driven through the West End of London.

After World War I there was a very noticeable lack of young men, the middle and upper classes having suffered appalling losses. With patriotic fervour they had left home to fight 'the war to end all wars' only to be slaughtered in their thousands. Young men who might have been partners for Katy and Connie, not to mention prospective husbands, were all dead.

From the age of fifteen, Edward was much in demand as an escort for Katy and Connie. The girls did not like going to a dance hall on their own. His sisters taught him to dance so that once in a while they could have a male partner. He became adept at the one-step and the foxtrot. They frequently went to small local dances. The demand for suitable space was so great that the seats would be taken out of a cinema in order for it to be used for dancing. Sometimes the extent of Edward's involvement was to see Katy and Connie inside the door of a dance hall before going off on his own pursuits. If no man were available, the girls danced with each other.

Katy and Connie insisted that their brother be suitably attired to take them to a dance. One night when he was to escort them to a special event, he was sporting a big black eye from a boxing bout the night before. During the day the bruise around his eye had matured and when he appeared at dinner, it was in full, colourful splendour. His sisters were horrified.

"Look at the state he's in. Look at his eye. We can't go with him looking like that!"

They didn't go to the dance.

When the season ended at Covent Garden Opera House, the seats were removed and the space rented out as a dance hall. Two bands would play, one at either end of the floor, since there was no amplification. Kiosks dispensing food and drinks and some even offering haircuts, were set up around the sides. Whole families came, from young children to old people. Teams of young couples, eight or nine year olds, boys in tails, the girls in long dresses, gave display dances. Professionals gave exhibition dances. There were competitions. Dancing became something of a national obsession.

One night Edward went in with Katy and Connie to Covent Garden and sat down to talk with the family of a young woman who often came to his father's shop. His sisters came over.

"Hold our handbags, Edward, while we dance."

At the end of the evening Katy and Connie were nowhere to be seen. He waited and waited but when they didn't appear, he assumed they had left with someone else. Highly embarrassed at having to carry their handbags, he finally left, travelled home and went to bed. When Katy and Connie returned hours later he was fast asleep. They burst into Edward's room.

"We're going to kill you. Why did you leave without us?"

"I thought you'd already left," was Edward's feeble response.

"Idiot! Of course we wouldn't have left without our handbags. We were in the toilet. There was a long queue."

"We had to walk almost all the way. We had no money for the train."

As Edward cowered under the blankets, they advanced upon his bed, grabbed the mattresss and turfed him onto the floor before storming from the room.

Alice Anstey, 1924

SISTERS AND SPORTS

We were all so different but I was very fond of my sisters. Katy was the brilliant one and Connie was terribly eccentric. They were both very kind. Dorothy and I were the two who were into sports.

Elizabeth's death in 1925 had desolated the whole family. Edward and his sisters all withdrew a little into themselves, becoming very private people. After work they immersed themselves in their separate interests; Katy in her writing, Connie in looking after Bobby, and Edward and Dorothy with sports. In their fear of the dreaded tuberculosis they all became fervent devotees of fresh air and exercise.

The three girls each had secretarial jobs - there was very little choice of occupation for women. Katy worked for a publisher and had several short stories and poems of her own published in magazines. She had a wicked wit and wrote scurrilous verse about everyone she knew. At Sunday dinners she regaled the family with her pieces. She took French classes at night school and attended political meetings to support the cause of the suffragettes. Then tuberculosis began to take its toll, eating away at her lungs, sapping her strength.

Katy, like her mother, had been sick for years before she died in 1931 at the age of thirty-three. She was tall, had her mother's brown eyes and wore her hair short. Katy was clever and vivacious and loving and the family was proud of her. But when she started to complain of always being tired, some days unable to go to work, they recognized with dismay that she, like Kathleen before her, had tuberculosis.

Gradually Katy relinquished more and more of her activities until finally she had to give up work. She developed a high fever and coughed incessantly. When her sisters and brother saw the blotches of bright arterial blood on her handkerchiefs, it was obvious she was doomed. They all knew by heart the symptoms of tuberculosis.

Katy fought hard to live. She tried anything recommended as a cure for consumption. She drank vile concoctions - iodine, salts of mercury, copper, and more - which were supposed to cure, but to no avail. The doctor prescribed a regimen of fresh air so a hut was built for her halfway down the long garden. On three sides the walls reached to the roof. The wall on the side facing the house reached only halfway. Inside the hut there was just room for a cot. After sitting over a hot fire all evening Katy would steel herself to go out to a cold, damp bed to sleep. But nothing she did halted the inexorable progress of the disease.

The gas mantle in Edward's room overlooking the garden had broken and not been replaced. Nothing was ever fixed in the Coppard house. A naked jet of lighted gas burned as the curtains flapped by the open window. No matter what the weather, Edward always slept with his window wide open. He had fallen asleep and woke to hear Katy's weak voice from the garden below,

"Edward, Edward, the curtains are on fire!"

Edward leaped out of bed, ripped down the curtains and threw them out of the window. They landed on the tree under his bedroom. The tree burst into flames, blazing with a great rushing sound. Exploding branches filled the air. Connie and Dorothy woke up and rushed into Edward's room to see what was happening. They leaned over the sill, laughing. Katy looked up at her brother and sisters and smiled but she had no breath for laughter.

Papa came out of his bedroom and roared,

"What in hell is going on?"

Edward was fixated by the vision of his father's white legs beneath his nightshirt. It was the first time he had ever seen Papa's legs and he couldn't believe how pallid they were. For a moment he couldn't speak.

"It's the tree, the tree, Papa, but it's alright now. The fire's out."

The blaze had consumed the tree and the excitement was over. Edward, Connie and Dorothy stood at the window in silence, grieving for their dying sister, looking at her with compassion as Katy walked slowly down to her cold hut. Then they all went back to their warm beds.

For more than two years, Katy survived the rigours of the garden hut. When it became obvious that she hadn't much longer to live Katy stayed indoors. She was given oxygen. At night Connie or Dorothy stayed up to administer the oxygen. Someone was with Katy always. She could not speak. Married by then, living in his own flat, Edward came each evening after work and sat beside her, observing the pulse in her neck, watching her struggle to breathe. Seeing his beloved sister's agony, Edward thought,

'At least Mama was spared this.'

Katy endured a week, watched over by her family, and then she died.

When Elizabeth was sick Connie had helped by looking after Bobby. Connie became Bobby's second mother, kind and gentle. With her friends she took him on Saturday shopping expeditions. While they debated the purchase of a new dress, Bobby danced impatiently outside the shop.

They went for train rides into the country, to Otford or Shoreham or Aylesford and took long walks before returning home. Connie was never very athletic and it wasn't hard for her to match her stride to the slower pace of a little boy.

Bobby loved train rides, watching the houses whiz by, seeing the doll-people in their gardens. Then the houses gave way to fields and trees and cows. When Connie and Bobby arrived at their station, they clambered down the steep steps onto the platform ready to begin their walk.

On one expedition Boris, a middle-aged banker, accompanied them. Bobby's gaze was drawn from the window to Boris' enormous, fat hands which seemed to touch Connie a great deal. When Boris leaned over and patted Bobby on the head, saying,

"You're a very good, quiet little boy," Bobby flinched. Bobby's private name for Boris was Frankenstein. That night when Connie bathed him and put him to bed as usual, he said,

"I don't like Boris, Connie."

"Neither do I, Bobby. I'm not seeing him again."

Connie was a fanatic about fresh air. Summer and winter alike the last thing she did before leaving Bobby's room at night was to throw the sashed window up as far as it would go. Sometimes she took him to the pictures and then in the middle of the film she'd get to her feet, exclaiming,

"I've got to have some air!"

She made her way to the aisle, stumbling over people's feet, causing a commotion, leaving Bobby cowering in his seat, highly embarrassed. After ten minutes or so, she would return.

In the evenings, while the others were out, Connie indulged her hobby of knitting. She was an expert knitter and made stylish sweaters, cardigans and even dresses for the family.

Dorothy was a versatile, powerful swimmer. She dived,

played water polo for England and was one of the best swimmers in the country. In the evenings and at weekends, she would go off to a swimming gala or competition, win medals and plaques, come home and casually toss her spoils into a drawer.

Having become interested in water polo, she pioneered this sport for women. With her expertise and enthusiasm she did a great deal to popularize the sport. It became viable for women to play and to be taken seriously. Dorothy was captain of Kent's Ladies' water polo team and after the first intercounty water polo match between Kent and Sussex the local paper reported:

Kent had a telling advantage with... their captain, playing centre forward. Her fast swimming, strong throws and general experience of the game, put her streets ahead of any other player in the water...She it was who scored all four goals…. Beckenham Advertiser

Swimming galas were very popular, attracting hundreds of spectators. The programme would include a number of different events: swimming, diving, water polo matches and aquatic displays.

Miss Coppard imitated a porpoise, and a submarine, besides waltzing in the water. . . . Beckenham Advertiser

Edward, at twenty, was five foot ten in height, had a good physique and was very fit. Shy green eyes hid behind the thick lenses of steel-rimmed glasses. A straight nose and regular features made him very handsome. His interest in people and quick repartee made him popular with the customers at Ted's fish shop.

Edward loved athletics and sport. He worked long hours for his father but some days took extended lunch hours when he would go to Stamford Bridge running track to train. He joined the boxing club at the Borough Polytechnic, going there to box and wrestle in the evenings. Wednesday night was wrestling: 'Catch as Catch Can', as it was called. Friday night was boxing. Because of his poor sight, Edward had to get in close to his opponent and so became an aggressive boxer. The amateur boxing matches consisted of three two-minute rounds with a minute between each round. Edward entered two matches but Ted would not watch him fight. He asked his friend, Bill,

"Will you go to see Edward fight? That Joe Drabinsky'll make mincemeat of him. I don't want to watch."

The first fight Edward won on points. In the second fight he did better and knocked his opponent out in the second round. Next morning, in Draper Street Market, everyone patted him on the back and congratulated him.

"Well done, Edward. Bill tells us you knocked Drabinsky out last night."

"I was very glad I was in the Catch-Weight division (10½ stone to 11½ stone) or I'd have been fighting that Irishman, McGinnis, and probably had my head knocked off."

" Showed Ted you 'ad it in yer, eh?"

"I 'ear you put up a really good show."

"Go' a gold medal, too, eh?"

Boxing was a very popular sport in London, especially South London. Every self-respecting young Cockney boy in the Elephant and Castle knew how to box and hoped that if he were good enough he could make enough money to have a better life. They boxed in the ring at Blackfriars, once a circular chapel. Another popular ring was Premierland, which the Jewish fraternity patronized. A working-class man wasn't much interested in other sports, nor, in any event, would he have had opportunity to pursue such an involvement.

Boxing was a favourite spectator sport even among

intellectuals - Bernard Shaw among them - and the crowds wanted their money's worth. They expected to see plenty of action followed by a knockout blow.

But Edward's heart was never in boxing. He preferred to keep fit with swimming, running, long walks on Sundays, and tennis whenever he could.

Tennis was the game of the 1920s for the middle classes. Anyone who could afford the obligatory white flannels or tennis dress, a racquet and a pair of gym shoes, played tennis. Women could and did play. Tennis, like boxing, was a popular spectator sport and the old facilities at Wimbledon were no longer adequate for the crowds who wanted to watch.

In 1922, King George V had opened a new stadium which accommodated fifteen thousand people.

Dorothy came home one day in great excitement.

"I've got two tickets for Suzanne Lenglen. Coming with me, Edward? They'll be serving strawberries and cream, too."

Suzanne (as she was always called) Dorothy's idol, everyone's idol, was never defeated in a singles match. She was tall and slim and practically danced on the court. In order to have more freedom of movement, she dispensed with the long skirt and usually wore a short, loose-fitting dress and white stockings. Sometimes she wore a short pleated skirt with a sweater. Her hair was tied back in a brightly-coloured bandeau. All the women players at Wimbledon wore white stockings because Queen Mary, who was there with other members of the Royal Family day after day to watch the tennis stars, did not like to see bare legs.

Louie (Webber) Anstey, midwife, 1903

MARRIAGE

I was still very fond of Adèle but too shy to do anything about it. Then Alice asked me to a dance and Adèle was there, she looked at me, her eyes were daggers. She never forgave me.

When Alice's affair ended she turned to me. She decided I would do. And that's how it all started.

The General Strike, in May of 1926, was the means by which Alice Anstey and Edward Coppard renewed contact. When the Coppards moved from Avenue Road the families had lost touch although Alice knew where Ted's fish shop was.

A commission which had been looking into the coal mining industry had made various suggestions to improve the industry. Reorganization and improvements for the miners such as pithead baths were for the future; the commission's present recommendation was for reduced wages. The owners rejected any reorganization and wanted not only reduced wages but longer working hours.

The miners' spokesman replied:

"Not a penny off the pay, not a minute on the day."

On May 1 the miners were locked out. A national strike began on May 3 when transport and railway workers, printers, workers in heavy industry, building, and gas and electricity were called out. Workers were loyal to their unions whose objective was to get the government to negotiate over the coal industry.

Volunteer drivers for trains and lorries were recruited from ex-army officers and from the universities. Mass pickets in London's East End stopped and quite frequently wrecked vehicles suspected of carrying goods or office workers to and from the City. It became a class war.

Charles Anstey, Alice's father, was supervisor at the Elephant and Castle Post Office and during the strike when the trains weren't running, he drove his car to work. Alice rode with him so that she could also get to her job.

Alice had always wanted to be a physical education teacher, but her parents persuaded her to take secretarial courses after leaving school. Her first job was with the Waifs and Strays Society in London. Although she didn't enjoy secretarial work she felt great satisfaction when the life of a deprived child could be eased. Then her father suggested that she take the Civil Service examination. After passing this successfully, she got employment with the Public Works Loan Board, typing deeds for property. She hated this job, finding it too impersonal.

After finishing work one day during the strike Alice started walking towards the Post Office to wait for her father as arranged. A mass of silent, sullen men was blocking the pavement where she had to walk. Slowly Alice made her way through them.

A bus appeared, driven by a volunteer, a young university student. The double-decker bus he drove was open in front where the driver sat to operate the vehicle. Except for an overhang protecting him from a possible downpour he was exposed to the elements. The upper deck was open, but the main section for passengers was enclosed.

As the bus approached, an angry murmur rose from the men lining the pavements either side of the road. It was a menacing sound. The driver was young, slight, and had an impassive expression on his face. He looked neither left nor right; he kept his gaze straight ahead.

One after another, as the bus drew level with him, each man reached into his pocket, withdrew a stone and threw it at the driver. Alice stood still. She heard a *thwack* as a stone hit the young man. A cut opened on his forehead and blood ran down his face. Alice was frightened. She pushed her way through the throng and ran to Ted's shop in Draper Street.

"They're stoning a bus driver. I think they're going to kill him!"

Ted sent a young errand boy to the Post Office to tell Charlie that Alice would wait at the shop until he came for her. She was there for hours. Edward made good use of the time Alice waited at the shop, chatting her up in between serving customers.

Later that day, another bus which had been trying to dodge strike pickets at the Elephant and Castle crashed onto the pavement and killed a man. Mounted police broke up the angry crowd.

Nine days later the unions called off the general strike but the miners held out for six months. When, because they were starving, they had to go back to work, nothing had been gained. Nothing was done to improve working conditions. Indeed, they had to accept lower wages and longer hours.

Alice started going out with Edward. She was on the rebound from a previous relationship, having just parted company from a married man she had been seeing illicitly for a year. Edward was too shy to further his cause with Adèle and she had given up on him.

Alice took Edward in hand. She invited him to a dance at the Irish Club to which she belonged. Alice went often to the Coppard's house. Edward, however, never came to the Anstey's because Louie, Alice's mother, did not approve of him.

Lucretia (Louie) Webber's early life had been hard. Her father died when she was eleven, leaving her mother destitute with three children. Louie's mother was reduced to working as a barmaid, and Louie was put out to service. The wealthy family, for whom she worked as a maid, treated her well, however.

Her employers had a large number of children. Before the arrival of each new baby, a midwife was installed in the house to attend the birth and look after the infant. As she observed the midwife at work, Louie was filled with a burning ambition to become a midwife herself. She was fortunate to have the support of her employers. When she went for an interview at a London hospital, she was accepted for training as a nurse in spite of her lack of education. She achieved her goal and became a certified midwife.

For the first year she worked with poor people in the slums of Woolwich. Often when she came into the room where a woman was about to give birth, there would be no sign of a crib for the baby, let alone clothes for it.

"Have you a sheet? A blanket?" she would ask.

Sometimes she had to take a cover from off the bed. Then she took a drawer from a chest, removed its contents, and lined the drawer with the bed cover ready to receive the baby.

In one of these poor houses, a young girl told her that the people for whom she worked as a maid needed a midwife. Louie went for an interview and was hired. For several years she delighted in the status of her position as midwife in the houses of scores of wealthy clients.

At a garden party given by one of her patients, Louie met Charles Anstey who had come with his mother. Charles' father had died when he was twelve and Charles was a frequent escort for his charming, elegant mother. Charlie was impressed with the young woman who seemed to be held in high regard by her employers.

When Charlie and Louie married they received scores of lavish gifts from her clients. Louie enjoyed comfort and stability in her marriage to Charlie.

While she had no animosity towards Edward, Louie hoped for something better than a tradesman's son for her daughter.

Katy and Connie were avid theatre-goers. Sybil Thorndike was their idol and since seeing her performance in Shaw's Saint Joan, they had been to every play in which Thorndike had acted. Alice and Edward joined them. They saw Edith Evans and the young Laurence Olivier. They went to variety shows at the Elephant Theatre, an enormous place where the bar was open all the time, not just at intermission. When Alice became a member of the Crystal Palace Choir, Edward enjoyed going to her concerts. But her attempt to interest him in opera failed dismally when she took him to see a performance of Wagner's Lohengrin. He fell asleep.

Alice loved sports as much as Edward and thought that their shared interests in games and the theatre would be a good basis for marriage. She was delighted to be Edward's tennis partner and at the Coppard's house she and Edward often played table tennis.

Edward worked such long hours that they didn't see as much of each other as Alice would have liked so, in 1929, she began to make plans for a holiday with him. Summer holidays had always been part of the Anstey way of life. They decided to go to Wales. Alice had persuaded her father to lend her his car. He was under the impression that there would be a party of four going on holiday.

Edward spoke to Ted.

"I'd like a couple of weeks off for a holiday, Papa."

"Holiday! Holiday! What d'you want a holiday for?"

In the ten years he'd worked for his father, Edward had never had a holiday; odd days off, but no more.

"Charlie will lend us his car; Reggie and I are going, and Alice and Mary."

Alice had coached him.

"Two weeks? Two weeks?"

Edward was persistent and Ted finally agreed. But as Edward and Alice planned to go alone they needed to be married. They were both virgins. Alice was headstrong but not imprudent. She suggested they get married secretly.

"Why keep it secret, Alice?"

"Because Mother wouldn't agree and there would be such a fuss."

"But Papa won't like it and —"

Edward lived in a house with three strong-minded sisters who bossed him and Alice was no different. She overrode his objections.

On the morning of July 29, Alice left her house wearing a pale green dress with a coat of the same colour over it, white gloves and shoes and a hat. She hated hats but felt that this occasion demanded one. Alice had classic features: a perfectly oval face, fine straight nose, large brown eyes and a dimple in her chin. With her wavy brown hair framing her face she was beautiful.

At the registry office, Alice met Edward and his cousin, Vic, who had been sworn to secrecy. Edward wore a double-breasted pale grey suit with a silk hat. They made a handsome pair. A passerby was brought in to act as the second witness and they were married. Then they were off for two weeks together in North Wales.

When they returned Alice spent a lot of time at the Coppard house. People were always coming and going and she was sometimes able to creep up to Edward's room unobserved. But it wasn't long before Alice discovered that she was pregnant. All hell broke loose.

Alice told her parents.

"I knew you were married," declared Louie. "That day you got all dressed up I suspected you were up to something and I followed you. I saw you go into the registry office or I wouldn't have let you go away with Edward."

Edward told his father.

"Alice is pregnant and you expect me to believe that you were married in July?" screamed Ted.

"We *were* married."

"I'll be the laughing stock of the market. You tell them."

Edward attempted to explain to his uncles but made no headway at all.

"Couldn't wait, eh?"

"Married! Tell us another one!"

In the end Ted was forced to take the marriage certificate to show the skeptics at the market.

"Edward will be getting a rise now that we're married, won't he, Papa?"

Ted looked at his daughter-in-law with new respect. It was obvious he would not be able to bully her in the way he did his son. He gave Edward an increase in salary and the young couple got their own flat and set up house together. Their first daughter was born the following June. The doctor who had attended Alice asked her,

"What are you calling the baby? June, I suppose?"

"No," said Alice. "We're naming her Annette, but I like the name June. That can be her second name."

So, unlike her father, the baby was assured of a middle name.

Clare's arrival the following year was decidedly precipitate. Early one morning three weeks before the expected time of birth, Alice said to Edward,

"I think you'd better go and fetch Mother."

Edward sprinted the short distance to the Anstey's house

and returned very soon with Louie. They found Alice lying on the floor with a new baby girl beside her. Louie made sure that the infant was breathing, severed the umbilical cord, wrapped the baby up and laid her on a chair. Then she turned her attention to Alice while Edward went for the ambulance. As they were leaving for the nursing home, Louie said,

"That's it, have we got everything?"

"What about the baby?" asked Edward.

The flat was now patently too small for two adults and two babies so Charlie and Louie made the down payment on a semi-detached house in a new housing development for the young family. In 1932 West Wickham was a rapidly expanding village, ten miles south of London, struggling to acquire services and amenities as the population increased. A very effective Residents' Association was instrumental in getting trees planted on residential streets and train and bus services improved.

For Edward it was less than a mile to walk to the railway station where the train took him directly to London Bridge. Alice enjoyed being able to walk with her babies in a pram to nearby woods. West Wickham was a pleasant residential neighbourhood in which to bring up a family.

LOAMPIT VALE

Business in the Draper Street shop was as good as usual but at the end of the week there never seemed to be much money. I did not realize the extent of my father's gambling at the horse races nor how heavily he was drinking. It never occurred to me that my father might be an alcoholic.

The Wall Street crash on October 24, 1929 hurt British exports and shipping. Industries already having difficulties such as coal, iron and steel, shipbuilding and textiles were the most severely affected. By 1932, nearly one in four of the British labour force was out of work. Civil servants, teachers and police all took pay cuts. Protest marches continued.

The south of England was not affected to the same degree and Ted's business continued to do well although he was drinking heavily and gambling. Then he took a mistress and did not want his son around to witness his indiscretions. So in 1934, Ted bought a fish shop in Loampit Vale, Lewisham, in South London for Dad (Edward).

It was a disaster from the start. Dad discovered he had inherited outstanding debts to several wholesalers. Moreover, he had no experience with customers who expected credit. Some of them ran up huge tabs. Mother took on the bookkeeping and served in the shop occasionally, but they fell further and further behind financially.

Every morning Dad left very early for the market to buy the day's supplies. Along with the fish for the shop he'd often buy half a dozen big, fat Norwegian herring for us. Then we'd fry them and eat them with slices of bread and butter. We never had any money to spare but we ate well.

From the pavement one entered the shop where the fish was laid out on marble slabs. On one side were the dried fish, sausages and poultry. On the other side was the wet fish. At the end of each day Mother chose what she was going to cook for our dinner. Each night we had something different: plaice, sole, haddock, bream, herring, halibut, hake or skate, from the score or more different fish Dad sold in his shop. After Mother had made her selection, the rest of the unsold fish would be placed in the cooler at the back of the shop. The marble slabs were hosed down, the floor cleaned, and the shutters at the front pulled down.

A door at the back of the shop opened into an enclosed courtyard where Dad had his smokehouse, a brick enclosure. Inside, a row of haddock hung from a metal rod over smouldering oak sawdust. Smoked haddock was Dad's speciality as it was Ted's. Sunday morning breakfast was always smoked haddock with a poached egg on top. We all loved this special treat.

The oak sawdust was kept in a bin with a heavy wooden door which slid into position in front of it. The sawdust was very expensive and Clare and I were not allowed to go near it. One day, Clare, with the help of some friends, managed to lift the door and crawl inside the bin where they all had a great time throwing sawdust over each other. Then they'd had enough.

"Come on, Clare. I have to go."

"Help me lift the door, then."

They got it partway up and then the door crashed down onto Clare's foot. Her screams brought Dad and me running. He lifted the door and Clare and her friends crawled out of the bin. When he saw the state of his precious, expensive sawdust he was furious. I had rarely seen Dad angry. Clare's friends beat a hasty retreat and she sat on the ground, sobbing.

"Let's see your foot," said Dad. It was swelling alarmingly. "We'd better get that looked at."

He fetched the wheelbarrow, placed her in it and trundled her to the hospital where her foot was x-rayed. It was badly bruised but not broken. She was immobile for a week but did not receive a great deal of sympathy.

When an adjacent building was pulled down, rats moved from it into our shop. My parents bought a ferret which Dad brought home in a cage.

"What's his name, Dad?"

"Sam, his name's Sam."

Sam had beautiful gold-coloured fur and we admired his whiskers. During the day Sam was kept in his cage and at night was let out to hunt rats. In the morning a row of rats would be lined up on the shop floor for Dad to dispose of. Mother refused to go into the shop at night alone. In the rooms above, we encountered their smaller cousins, the mice.

Once when we were seated at the dining room table, Mother sent me to the kitchen for the jam which had been forgotten. I opened the cupboard door to see a small grey mouse sitting on top of the jampot, preening his whiskers. I screamed and he shot away. Mother came running.

"There was a mouse right there...."

"Well, I imagine he was a great deal more frightened of you than you were of him," she said matter-of-factly, and picked up the jampot.

The premises over the shop were a horror; dark and dingy and cramped. When Mother first saw where we were to live she sank into a chair and burst into tears. It was a terrible comedown from the house and surroundings she had so enjoyed in West Wickham. When we moved to the shop, the house in West Wickham was not sold, however. Her parents, Charlie and Louie, went there to live.

The rooms were accessed through the shop, then up a narrow, dark staircase onto a landing. A passageway led to the living/dining room on the right, facing the street and then the bedroom for us children. The kitchen and toilet and my parents' room were at the back. There was no bathroom. In the kitchen stood an old bathtub covered, when not in use, with a plank of wood. During the day the surface was needed for kitchen items. Whenever anyone had a bath the plank, with its accumulation of paraphernalia, had first to be removed.

Trams trundled incessantly past the shop. The walls vibrated and the plastered ceilings were constantly cracking and falling. One night, chunks of plaster landed on my bed as I lay asleep, narrowly missing my head. Clare and I started shouting. We were frightened. Mother came in, slapped the light on and looked at us through a cloud of dust.

Clare and I had strict instructions never to attempt to cross the street by ourselves. When we were ready for school we waited while Dad, in his white smock smeared with blood from the fish he had been filleting, advanced slowly into the street, arms extended above his head. When the traffic stopped we scuttled safely across. He watched for us on our return and went through the same procedure. Clare and I found this very embarrassing.

One day we saw a woman stumble and fall in front of a tram. Clare and I watched in horror as she was pulled under the wheels and dragged along until the tram came to a stop. Dad pushed us back into the shop and ran to see if he could help. She was dead. We did not go to school that day.

Once a week on Mondays, when trade was slow, Dad left the shop for his assistant to look after while he came to fetch us after school. Then we went to the swimming baths at Goldsmith's College where he taught us to swim. The water was always beautifully warm. This was the best day of the week. One day Dad lined us up at the side of the pool, poised to swim across by ourselves. He stood ready to dive to our aid if necessary, but was confident we were able to swim the width of the pool.

"I'll drown, Daddy, I'll drown!" Clare screamed.

I had already jumped in and started swimming. Dad picked Clare up, and dropped her in the water. She bobbed to the surface and beat me across. She did most things better than I did.

My youngest sister was born in 1937. Mother had allowed us to feel her growing belly and told us that we would soon have a brother or sister. Jennifer was duly born and we all delighted in her.

At school I became embroiled in a fierce argument.

"We have a new baby. She came out of my mother's tummy."

"Stupid, 'course she didn't. Everyone knows you get babies under gooseberry bushes."

"No you don't. They grow inside a mother's tummy."

"My mum got our brother under a gooseberry bush."

"Well, our baby came out of my mother's tummy. It's flat now the baby's come out."

This seemed to me irrefutable proof.

"How did it get out then?"

But this was beyond my scope.

"Anyway, we haven't got any gooseberry bushes in our yard," was my parting shot.

Christmas Day was always at Ted's house. Ted's brothers and sisters came with their children and it was crowded, noisy and fun. After dinner the children were all packed away into bedrooms while the adults continued to party. Every year they played a noisy card game, where they all screamed for what seemed like hours: one-one-one, two-two-two, three-three-three. I lay in the room, listening to the noise, feeling left out, wishing I was old enough to join in the fun. Years later I discovered that the name of the game was Pit.

The Christmas after the move to Loampit Vale, Mother decided to give Ted a piece of her mind. Fortified by several glasses of wine she began,

"The shop's a disgrace, Papa. It's fit only for rats and there are plenty of those. It's awful for the children. And we're losing money. You should never have put Edward there."

Papa continued carving the turkey and ignored this barb.

"Would you like the Parson's nose, Alice?" he asked, knowing she had a penchant for it.

After dinner he made sure she had her favourite liqueur, cherry brandy. But he never admitted any responsibility for my parents' difficulties.

Mother and Dad could never afford a holiday, but one summer they sent Clare and me away with a group of children to the seaside for two weeks. The second day there I came down with chicken pox and was confined to a room by myself for the entire two weeks. The teachers would not let me read and I was bored to death. No one was allowed to visit me.

Back at home Clare came out in spots and then Mother became very sick with chicken pox, as adults sometimes do. At seven years old I was anxious to help.

"I can make toast and boil some eggs."

The eggs were bullets and the toast was charred. The kitchen filled with smoke and I was mortified.

"I like well-done toast," said Dad, and he ate the burnt offering.

Sometimes on weekends Clare and I visited our grandparents, Charles and Louie. Once when Grandad came in his car to fetch us there was a thick, yellow, paralyzing fog, known as a pea-souper. Clare and I sat silent and still and scared while Grandad leaned over the steering wheel and peered through the windshield. We inched our way through the strangely quiet roads. It took us two hours to travel the five miles to West Wickham.

During these years in the shop Dad pursued his interest in running as often as he could. He joined the Kent Athletic Club and in 1938 won the one-mile championship over a bumpy, rotten old course. He went to Goldsmith's College once a week for gymnastics. Hoping to be able to develop his interest in aeronautics he joined the Royal Air Force Reserves. Once in a while he escaped from the drudgery of the shop, but Mother rarely could.

By August of 1939, Dad was heavily in debt to several wholesalers. They refused him further credit and he had to close the shop. He received notice to appear in court to answer charges against him.

The lawyer representing the wholesalers gave his statement.

"Your honour, Mr. Coppard has failed to respond to our many requests for payment for goods received."

After listening to the case against Dad, the judge turned to him.

"What are you going to do about these debts, Mr. Coppard?"

"My shop is closed, your honour. I have been called to start training next week with the R.A.F. Reserves."

"If that be the case, I find these claims against you to be no longer valid. Case dismissed."

Dad felt an overwhelming relief.

"Thank you, your honour."

He left for his training and in less than a month Clare and I were evacuated. We never did return to the shop. The blitz reduced it to rubble.

CONSCRIPTION

People are fascinating. I've always enjoyed being in the role of observer, standing on the sidelines, watching people, their actions, their foibles. I found this technique very useful in the R.A.F. It helped me avoid some unpleasant situations.

Signs of impending war became ever more visible. Gas masks had been issued, trenches dug in public parks, Anderson shelters delivered. These shelters were made of corrugated iron, buried to a depth of four feet in people's gardens, and covered with at least fifteen inches of soil.

On August 11, 1939, Dad joined his R.A.F. Reserve Unit for what was to be a month's training. But when war was declared on September 3, the one month he'd expected to be away extended into six long years of service in the R.A.F.

Registration for conscription started with the youngest age group. In theory, the recruit could choose which of the three Armed Forces he wished to join. But the manpower of the Royal Navy, most conscripts' first choice, was smaller than the other two. Most recruits ended up in the army.

The R.A.F. was first choice for those young men hoping to be, if not pilots, at least part of an aircrew. They came from small villages, large towns, different backgrounds, all thrown together to be moulded into a working unit.

Rumours abounded:

"The doctors are all queers."

"If you get sent to the glasshouse they make you sleep standing up."

Medical examination for rupture or venereal diseases was known as a 'short arm' inspection. The men would be formed up in a line, with their trousers loosened ready to drop once they were in front of the doctor. Dad decided that this was one procedure he would avoid if at all possible; indeed, during all his time in the Air Force he managed never to submit to what he considered an indignity. He always joined the lineup as required. Then at a strategic moment as the queue edged towards the doctor he dropped out of the line. He would take a few steps back, start pulling his trousers up as if his examination were over, slowly walk to the back of the room and then nip out of the exit door.

Fearful tales were told of the military prison known as the glasshouse - so called because it had a glass roof. Airmen who committed serious misdemeanours were sent there. A man was kept moving from the time he put his feet to the ground in the morning to the time he fell exhausted into bed at night. Every activity was timed, including the three S's - shaving, showering, and shitting. If a man had to crap at any other time he was required to keep his feet beating as he sat on the pot.

Chaps would collapse after doing interminable pushups.

"Lift your arse up. Lift *anything* up!"

After an hour of running round the square,

"Do another five minutes."

Then, "Now, on the double round the square again!"

One inventive sergeant devised an activity for his unfortunate victims. A heap of coal was kept in the corner of one cell with a bucket of whitewash and brush beside it.

"See that pile of coal there? Move each piece to that corner opposite."

There was no shovel provided. Half an hour later the sergeant would return.

"Right! Now whitewash that dirty corner."

It went on, back and forth, all day.

After thirty days in the glasshouse, airmen would return to their unit with shaven head, hollow cheeks and shaking legs. The recidivism rate was low.

Dishwashing was the most despised chore in camp but each time a group of fresh recruits arrived, the sergeant was assured of a new lot of dishwashers. When he came into the Nissen hut the morning following the arrival of a new contingent, he said,

"Anyone for late breakfast? Who'd like a late breakfast? You'll do me a big favour. We can't seat everyone in one go."

The new recruits fell over themselves volunteering for the privilege. No one questioned why none of the seasoned airmen evinced the slightest interest in having a late breakfast.

"Thank you, lads, thank you," said the sergeant as he took note of their names, "when you've done, just make sure you come and see me."

As the newcomers left the canteen after their leisurely, late breakfast, the sergeant was waiting for them.

"Come with me, lads. I've got a small job for you."

They followed him into the kitchen where they were confronted by a mound, from floor to ceiling, of dirty dishes.

"There you are, lads. Look lively and get that lot cleared up quickly. You'll be on this detail for a week."

As everyone shook down into life in the R.A.F. a rough compassion was shown by the older men towards some of the unseasoned young recruits. Tommy, a shy eighteen-year-old, short, baby faced, bespectacled, away from home for the first time, was in a perpetually dazed state.

His first night out in a pub with the boys he was desperate to prove himself. Tommy did his best to keep up with the others' fast-paced drinking.

"Time to go, Tommy."

Tommy stood up and promptly fell back into his seat. Dad and his friend, James, grabbed him, one on each arm, and made their way back to camp. Seated on his cot in the Nissen hut, Tommy immediately threw up all over the floor.

"Christ, what a mess!"

James and Dad cleaned it up, stripped Tommy's clothes off and got him into bed where he sank into a stupor. Then an appalling stench arose and it was obvious that Tommy had soiled himself. This was too much. James and Dad looked at each other from their cots either side of Tommy. Dad inclined his head, indicating the door. James nodded. They roused the two men opposite, gestured towards Tommy, motioned again in the direction of the door and then each man moved towards a corner of Tommy's cot, lifted it, and carried it out of the hut watched by twenty pairs of eyes. No one spoke. Tommy's cot was deposited a good way from the hut in the middle of a field.

Next morning, the sergeant came into the hut on his usual mission:

"Rise and shine! Hands off your joysticks. Look lively!"

Then he noted the missing cot. He turned on his heel, strode back to the doorway and looked out to see Tommy sitting up in his cot, completely bewildered.

The hapless Tommy seemed quite unable to adjust to life in the Air Force. It was all too much for him. Trouble dogged his footsteps and he was an easy target for despotic sergeants. Dad tried to give him a few pointers.

"If you want to stay out of trouble, take time to assess a situation before you enter the scene. Then endeavour to look busy. If you've nothing to do, invent something. Pick up a bucket and walk with it someplace, any place. Never draw attention to yourself."

Unfortunately for Tommy he was unable to heed this last piece of advice in the matter of the greatcoat. Standard equipment issued to all recruits included a greatcoat. On Saturday nights chaps with passes used to frequent the local dancehall. They were much in demand as men were in short supply. One Saturday night Dad sneaked out without a pass. He anticipated no problem getting back into camp as James was on sentry duty. At the end of the dance Tommy rushed up to him.

"Ed, I can't find my greatcoat!"

Dad looked at the heap of greatcoats through which Tommy had been searching and figured it would be hopeless to try and identify Tommy's coat from the mass on the floor. Besides, Dad had to be back at camp before James went off duty.

"Take one, any one."

Tommy grabbed a coat and ran after Dad who was already jogging down the road back to camp.

Next morning Tommy stood on parade in full kit as required. On his face was a look of abject misery. The sergeant advanced down the line of men standing to attention until he stood in front of Tommy. Tommy's greatcoat enveloped him completely and his hands could not be seen.

"Whose coat is that?'

"Mine, sir."

This response did not justify any comment. Tommy was marched away, the greatcoat sweeping the ground as he walked.

Clare and Annette, Ringmer, Sussex, 1939

EVACUATION

Ringmer was a stupid place for children to be sent, just eight miles from the south coast. If the Germans HAD invaded England, you'd have been right in the thick of it. But of course we didn't know your destination when you set off.

An extraordinary occurrence took place in Britain in the weeks before the war began. Because it was feared that the cities, and London in particular, would be the focus of heavy bomb attacks, more than three and a half million people moved to the countryside. People with means took themselves; others were part of the government's evacuation plan. Under the government scheme, school children with their teachers, mothers with pre-schoolers, elderly and handicapped people were all evacuated.

This incredible exodus took place between June and September. Clare and I were two of thousands of school-aged children evacuated from urban London to rural England on September 1, 1939, two days before Britain declared war on Germany. We had been rehearsed for the event several times, going to the school in readiness to leave for an unknown destination. We had gas mask drills. We overheard adults talking.

"London will be bombed."

"Best to make sure the children are safe."

"You're going to be evacuated," Mother told us.

"Evacuated? What's that?"

"You're going away into the country."

"Aren't you coming?"

"No. Jennifer and I are going to stay with Grannie and Grandad in West Wickham."

In theory, at least, we were prepared.

We set off that morning for the train station, with our nametags pinned to our chests, gas masks slung round our necks, and small suitcases in our hands. I was very impressed with my 'evacuation' blanket, a multicoloured, thin cotton blanket which was to stay with me throughout the war years. We had no idea where we were going. Parents were to be informed of their children's whereabouts when they reached their destination. Grannie, Mother and Jennifer were with us to see us off.

When we arrived at the station we made our way through the throng on the platform to join our classmates. I had never seen so many people in one place before. Out of seeming chaos, tight clusters of children gradually formed with their teachers in the centre of each group. Anxious parents hovered on the periphery. No child shouted; no child ran. It was strangely quiet.

I looked at Grannie who was silently crying, big tears rolling down her cheeks, and at Mother who was holding Jennifer. Suddenly I felt very frightened. Dad had gone, left us, and now Clare and I were to leave Mother and Jennifer. Theory became reality; an explanation was comprehended. The cloud of fear hanging over the crowd, born of all our uncertainties, was palpable.

The train came in and we all piled on, directed by our teachers.

"Be good," were my grandmother's last words to us.

As the train pulled out of the station, Jennifer's wistful little face faded away.

On board the train, Miss Ellery took charge. We chanted

times tables and the fields flew by. She pulled our gaze back from hills and streams as we repeated after her Kipling's words:

Land of our birth, we pledge to thee
Our love and toil in the years to be;
When we are grown and take our place,
As men and women with our race.

She was indefatigable; a stern, grey-haired woman in her habitual grey skirt doing her duty in an unprecedented situation. If a child faltered with a response she had her ruler ready to rap his or her knuckles. But with each mile of track, her power waned. One by one her charges slipped out of her reach, overcome by fatigue. Many of the children had been too nervous or excited to sleep the night before.

We finally arrived at Lewes, in Sussex, where we transferred onto buses for the last stage of our journey to the little village of Ringmer. Strange that we should land up there, just three miles from where our Coppard forebears had lived in Lewes.

At the village we all poured out of the buses into the hall where people who were to billet us awaited. Anyone who had a spare room was required to take one or two evacuees. Whereas at the station everything had been orderly, here there was confusion. Teachers with lists called names, trying to match children with requests from villagers for a particular age or sex. The village organizer had a list of billets available. Prospective hosts stood around the walls waiting to see what kind of child was going to be coming into their home.

Miss Ellery's voice could be heard above the Babel:

"Annette, Clare, stand over here. Mrs. Bourn has said she wants two girls of eight or nine so I think you will do. You will wait here until she comes for you."

We did as she directed and stood, holding hands, watching the scene in front of us.

The noise in the hall grew louder and louder. Older boys, released from the restraints of the train, jostled each other; played tag around small groups of younger children. When an assignment of a five or six-year-old was made to a billet, the child would be upset at leaving the relative security of the teacher. If a very young child had to abandon an older brother or sister whom their host didn't want they screamed in panic. Often an altercation would ensue.

"Me Mam told me I weren't to leave Billy. I want to go with him!"

"I'm sorry. This lady only wants a *little* boy."

We stood waiting for what seemed like hours. Every time the door of the hall opened and a woman appeared, I thought:

'Is that Mrs. Bourn?'

Gradually the hall cleared and Mrs. Bourn still had not come.

"Where is she, Annette?"

"I don't know."

"Maybe she won't come. What'll happen to us?"

Clare had verbalized my own fears and I said angrily,

"Of course she'll come."

A woman hurried into the hall.

"Where are my two little girls?"

Two pairs of eyes focused on her. She was a large, tall woman with fly-away, jet-black hair, a round, red-complexioned face and vivid blue eyes. She wore a bright red blouse, green trousers and Wellingtons, knee-high rubber boots. She was an extraordinary sight but then we didn't know that she had just come from working on a farm.

"Are you Mrs. Bourn?" asked Miss Ellery.

"Yes, are these the girls?"

As Mrs. Bourn came towards us, Clare and I burst into tears. The relief was overwhelming. We weren't going to be homeless after all.

Eva Bourn was determined to do well by us but she had no children of her own and no idea how to handle us. She told us to call her Auntie Bourn. She found our constant chatter irritating. When it became too much for her, she would say,

"Here's a farthing each. Go buy a gobstopper."

Off we would run to the shop. When in the mouth a gobstopper rendered one incapable of speech. After a few sucks it could be taken out and examined to see what colour had appeared. More energetic sucking would then uncover the next colour. A gobstopper was guaranteed to keep us occupied and relatively quiet for half an hour. Relishing our power, we exploited her shamelessly.

Mrs. Bourn was crude. At supper in the kitchen, she said,

"Who farted?"

No one we knew asked questions like this. When she got no response she came behind us and lifted up our skirts to sniff for the culprit.

Mrs. Bourn was also kind. When she discovered that we did not have any plimsolls for country dancing she took us on the bus into Lewes and bought us each a pair. Friday night was the night when villagers and evacuees gathered in the village hall for country dancing.

"Get your plimsolls on, girls; time to dance."

Off we went. I watched, fascinated, as the villagers danced. Then each of the adults took a child in tow and showed us the steps and movements - back-to-back, siding, arming, figure eights. We learned all the wonderful English country dances: Goddesses, Sellenger's Round, Gathering Peascods and Friday night became the highlight of the week for me.

Arthur Bourn was a farm labourer. He was a quiet, self-effacing man completely dominated by his large, loud wife. We liked him because when he got home from a long day in the fields he always had time to talk to us. He had no preconceived notions as to what a child should or should not do. He accepted us as we were. On our travels exploring the countryside, we watched him carving neat furrows in the ground after a crop had been harvested. One day he noticed us standing by the hedge.

"I'll give you a ride."

He stopped the tractor for us to clamber up beside him. As we bumped along, I looked back, marvelling at the straight lines emerging as the blades turned the soil.

There were tremendous thunder storms such as we had never experienced in London. The whole sky would be covered with a network of interlaced lines and then would come a great clap of thunder. As the echoes died away over the hills we would wait for the next flash of lightning to trace a different pattern in the sky.

Mrs. Bourn made wine. That glorious autumn we picked buckets and buckets of dandelions, elderberries and blackberries for her. It was not a chore for us; we relished the freedom of the countryside after the restraints of the city.

School hours were short because we had to share space and time with our country classmates. We had unprecedented freedom. Mrs. Bourn made one admonition:

"You stay together now, and be home for tea."

Having said that, her duty by us was done. We roamed for miles on the chalky downs, introducing ourselves to sheep and rabbits. We rolled over and over down the sloping hills, screaming in delight. We lay on our backs watching clouds scud across the sky. It was a new world; it was intoxicating.

My beloved books were forgotten for a while.

At night, lying in bed, Clare and I talked for hours.

"What'll Jennifer be doing without us?"

"I miss her."

"D'you think she still knows our names?"

"I wonder if she's talking now."

Mother had written to tell us that after we left, Jennifer had stopped talking. For weeks she had remained silent and sad.

"What do you think Dad's doing?"

Dad wrote us long letters.

"I'm training to be a flight mechanic. We have to make sure that the planes are safe for the pilots to fly...."

"When I come home, I'll take you both swimming again...."

Mother sent a parcel for us every so often with sweets enclosed. One day a parcel arrived when Mrs. Bourn was out. We ripped the wrapping off and there was a one pound slab of milk chocolate.

"Let's not tell Auntie Bourn. She'll just give us one piece every day. Let's have a feast tomorrow."

Excitedly we stuffed the slab of chocolate behind the dresser in the kitchen.

Next morning we waited and waited for Mrs. Bourn to leave the kitchen so that we could retrieve our booty. Then she started cleaning the floor. As she made her way towards the dresser we became more and more anxious.

"What's this?"

She pulled out the bar of chocolate.

"Did you put it there?"

I nodded mutely.

"Where did it come from?"

"We found it."

"Found it? Where?"

"In the fields."

She got to her feet, holding the chocolate out in front of her as if it were contaminated.

"In the fields?" Her voice rose. "Just the thing the Germans would do. Drop poisoned sweets for children."

She walked over to the range, lifted the lid and dropped the chocolate in.

After Germany took over Norway and Denmark in April of 1940, it was feared that England would be invaded. Along the coast from Norfolk to Sussex a ten-mile zone was designated from the coast inland. Our village fell within that space and plans were made to re-evacuate children to Wales. Mother decided that we would take our chances together and so we came back home. The bombardment of London had not taken place when expected, but was about to happen. Clare and I came home in time for the Blitz.

THE BLITZ

We were doing our level best to keep the planes aloft so that the pilots could fight off the German bombers. Those young men flew hour after hour, day after day - beyond the point of exhaustion. Dear old London. She sure took a beating.

Clare and I were not the only ones who came back home from being evacuated. Children from South and East London returned in the thousands. Their parents, contrary to what the planners of the mass evacuation had supposed, had not been happy at parting from their children. When no air raids had taken place as predicted, the children came back.

The East End of London, stretching along the Thames for six miles and inland for a depth of three miles was one of the worst slum areas in the western world. Between the wars various schemes had been undertaken to improve things, but the root cause, poverty, had not been addressed. So no headway was made. However, the 'phony war' was now over and the Blitz was about to demolish many of the slums. Many of those who were made homeless never did come back to the East End.

In July 1940, the Battle of Britain began. As Hitler stepped up his campaign to annihilate the R.A.F. Fighter Command as a necessary prelude to his planned invasion of Britain, we witnessed more and more aerial activity. Within viewing distance of the action in the skies over Biggin Hill Airport we watched encounters between German and British planes. We followed many a dogfight between Messerschmits and Spitfires, sometimes directly overhead, cheering whenever an enemy plane was chased off or shot down.

Dad was stationed at Kenley Airfield, not too far away. He worked as an aircraft mechanic. During the Battle of Britain the ground crews were frantically busy, refuelling and repairing planes between sorties. As the conflict intensified, ground crews and pilots alike were perpetually exhausted. When a Spitfire came to a stop one day at the airfield, no one climbed out.

"Something's wrong!" shouted Dad to the other ground staff.

They ran over and Dad climbed up onto the wing. The pilot was fast asleep. Sometimes the pilots were so worn out, they fell asleep as they ate.

A serviceman normally got about one week's leave every three months, but in these frenetic times Dad was lucky to get even a couple of days at home in August. Clare and I hadn't seen him since he had left a year before. We greeted him with delight and thought he looked very smart in his uniform with shiny brass buttons. His peaked cap was set at a jaunty angle aslant his head.

"Clare, you're as tall as Annette now!"

I had been hoping that no one would notice.

"It's not fair. She's a year younger than me."

As the battle in the skies escalated we learned to identify the different aircraft.

"See the glazed nose of the Heinkell, there? That's one of theirs."

We became adept at recognizing the different planes before we saw their identification marks. The Spitfires were our favourites; they moved with such speed and panache.

We watched in awe one day in August when nine Dornier 17s swept in to bomb the airfield at Biggin Hill. They were intercepted by two Hurricane squadrons and a great fight ensued. Two of the Dorniers were downed and the rest were driven off. Throughout that month the Luftwaffe launched a thousand planes a day across the channel. On August 15, they mounted their maximum effort with eighteen hundred sorties. The skies seemed always to be filled with planes and the noise was tremendous. It was a different world from the peaceful skies of Sussex we had known.

In September Clare and I started back to school at Hawes Down Junior. If the air raid siren sounded while school was in session, we picked up our books and marched down the steps into the underground shelter to continue our work. The light was dim and when winter came it was bitterly cold with water running down the bare brick walls. A dank smell permeated everything. Air raids were frequent. One day we went to the shelter three times.

In the classroom I was always able to keep my eyes on the book under my desk instead of the arithmetic I was supposed to be doing. In the shelter we sat on long benches lining the walls. I had no option but to do the hated arithmetic.

"Pay attention, Annette, you've got to be ready for your exam in March."

Mr. Dixon was doing his best to prepare us for the 'eleven-plus' exams to be written the following year. I was trying for a place at Beckenham Grammar School for Girls. I had made this my first choice since it was where Mother had been a student when the school first opened in 1919. A scholarship would enable me to have the sort of education which my parents could not have afforded.

If there was an air raid at night and the all clear sounded before midnight then school was open as usual next day. If the raid occurred after midnight, school was closed. Mother always sent us to school. Several times Clare and I walked the mile to school, only to find it closed. Once the school was closed for two days because of an unexploded bomb in The Mead, a nearby street. It was all very stressful and confusing. As the assaults on London escalated, we ceased going to school very much at all.

The Blitz began in earnest that Autumn. For fifty-six nights in a row London was bombarded from dusk to dawn. On September 7, hundreds of bombers targeted the London docks, setting them ablaze, lighting the way for more destruction throughout the night. We lay listening to wave after wave of bombers passing overhead. The racket of the anti-aircraft barrage was tremendous, but we found it comforting. The noise gave us the impression that something, at least, was being done to deter the bombers. Because of the din we couldn't hear the noise of the bombs whistling down, but neither could we sleep. The morning after a raid, Clare and I would rush outside to pick up pieces of shrapnel. We vied with each other to see who had the more interesting shapes of metal in our collections.

West Wickham didn't escape damage. A bomb fell in the High Street, completely demolishing one shop and damaging several others. Houses on residential streets were bombed. There was great excitement when a Messerschmit was shot down and the pilot captured.

On the afternoon of September 15, when every plane that the R.A.F. could muster was flown to fight off the Luftwaffe attacks on London, the Battle of Britain was on its way to being won. Two days later, Hitler postponed the invasion of Britain. It never did take place.

Dad, meantime, had been transferred to Kidbrooke, in South East London, to train as a balloon operator. Until Balloon Command was created, the vast majority of balloons had been manned by auxiliaries. During the Battle of Britain balloons were flown from barges and drifters in the Straits of Dover to protect shipping from low flying aerial attack.

'I wish I had a camera,' Dad wrote, 'you would be amazed at some of the antics these things get up to. They look like great whales floating up in the sky. Rumour has it that once we've finished training, we'll be heading north.'

During the Blitz, Grannie and Grandad lived with us in West Wickham. Our house in Bolderwood Way was a semi-detached with the front door on the side of the house, reached by a path alongside the lawn. Off the entrance hall was a small bedroom and a good-sized sitting room, both facing the street. A staircase opposite the front door led up to two bedrooms. To the left of the staircase, off the hallway, was a large dining room with French windows opening onto the back garden. On the opposite side of the passage were the toilet and bathroom. The kitchen was at the back. While my grandparents lived with us they had the front room to themselves.

In our dining room we had a Morrison shelter. It was like a steel table, and we slept underneath on a mattress. After a while we didn't even bother to go to our beds upstairs because we'd always have to come down to the shelter when the siren sounded. Night after night Clare and I lay either side of Jennifer as she cried in fright at the noise. It was okay to cry when you were only three. Clare and I were frightened, too, but we took comfort in the fact that we were all together.

Another 'safe' sleeping area was made in the big cupboard under the stairs which Grandad reinforced with solid wooden beams. An additional sleeping place was under the heavy oak dining room table. Along with the Morrison these places would have provided protection from falling debris had our house been damaged.

Grandad was not home very often at night. As an Air Raid

Precaution warden (known as the A.R.P.) dressed in uniform and tin hat, he was on duty at the Wardens' Post or patrolling the streets watching for fires, ready to help wherever there was a need. When there was a lull he slept in the wardens' hut.

Grandad wasn't always around when an incendiary bomb, a grey, cylindrical object about a foot long, landed. So Mother would dash out and extinguish the fire with a bucket of sand or soil which was always kept at hand. When one landed on the roof, Mother climbed a ladder, pole in hand, knocked it to the ground and extinguished the blaze. Then the Germans packed the incendiaries with an explosive charge and they became deadly. They had to be left to burn.

During the day Jennifer was Grandad's little shadow. She followed him wherever he went in her bright red siren-suit, a one-piece garment which Mother had made her.

"Where are you going, Grandad?"

"To the Wardens' Post."

"Can we come?"

It was quiet that day so he took us all to the post.

"Come on in. Would you girls like a cup of tea?"

"Yes, please."

Huts had been erected at intervals throughout the community, to be used as headquarters by the wardens. We investigated everything: the table and chairs, the camp beds, the telephone. We admired the teapot as we sat, on our best behaviour, drinking tea from an assortment of different coloured cups.

One day when Clare and I were at school, Jennifer set off by herself to visit Grandad. With her dolls' pram, her dolls comfortably arrayed inside, she set off for the Wardens' Post. Grandad was out on patrol so Jennifer was escorted home by two tall wardens, one on either side of her. The doorbell rang. Mother, who had just realized that Jennifer was missing, rushed to the door.

"Is this your daughter, Ma'am?"

Jennifer was bursting with excitement.

"My dollies and I had a lovely tea, Mother."

London got a temporary respite when the Luftwaffe began attacks on other areas of England and then one night in May 1941, the worst raid of all on London killed and injured more than three thousand people. Over two thousand fires were started. From ten miles away we could see London burning. As we looked at the red glow in the sky over the capital we wondered if there would be anything left of London at all. It took almost two weeks to put out the last of the fires.

In June, Hawes Down School received notification that six girls in our class had won scholarships to Beckenham Grammar School. I was one of them. Mother's immediate concern was how on earth she could get me the uniform I needed. She had no money. So she went to the shop.

"May I please borrow a tunic? I'll bring it back tomorrow."

Then she took it home and made a pattern from it so that she could buy some cheap material and make one.

But as it happened, I was not to start in September with the others. Dad wrote to say that he had found us a flat on the Firth of Forth, in Scotland, near where he was stationed.

Photograph courtesy of the Imperial War Museum, London

Supermarine Spitfires on patrol over Kent, summer of 1940

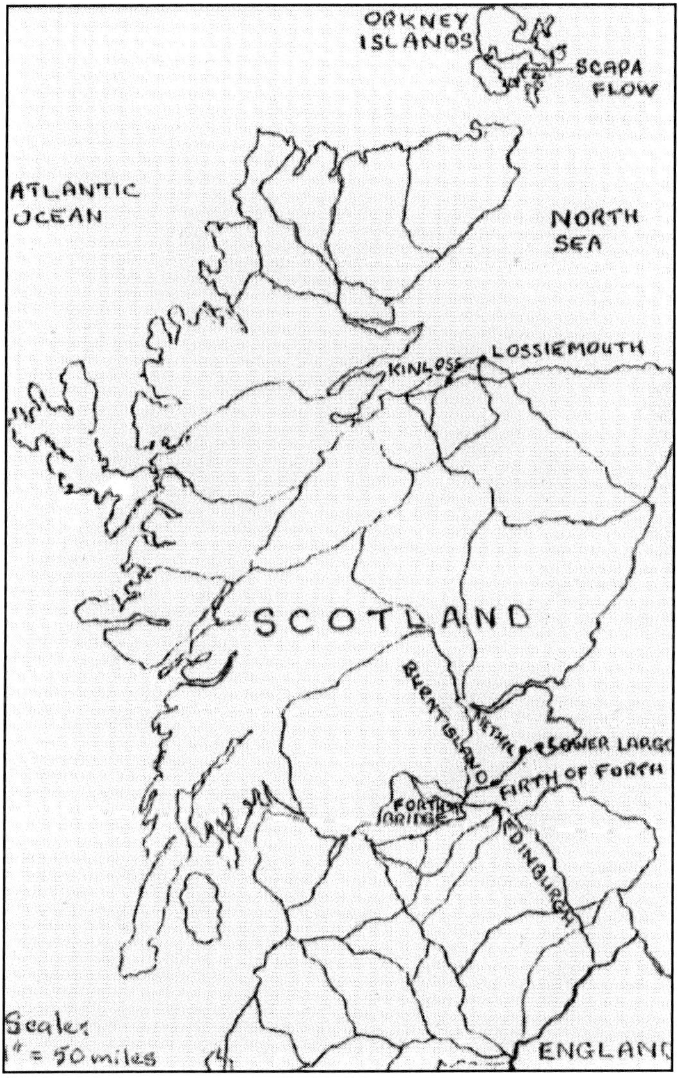
ORKNEY
ISLANDS
SCAPA
FLOW
ATLANTIC
OCEAN
NORTH
SEA
KINLOSS
LOSSIEMOUTH
SCOTLAND
BURNTISLAND
METHIL
LOWER LARG
FIRTH OF FORTH
FORTH
BRIDGE
EDINBURGH
Scale:
" = 50 miles
ENGLAN

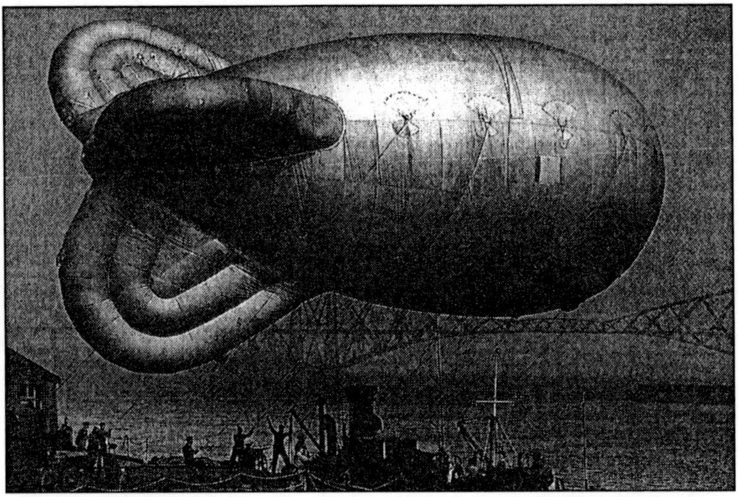

Photograph from 603 Squadron Archives

One of the balloons flown from a ship moored in The Firth of Forth

BALLOONS OVER THE FORTH

Even with the balloon floating above us, it was sometimes difficult to remember we were in the middle of a war. It was a beautiful place to be, sitting on a yacht anchored in the Forth.

In 1941, Dad was stationed at Burntisland on the Firth of Forth in Scotland. The area was under constant attack, mines being dropped most nights. Several ships were sunk and workcrews were kept frantically busy repairing the minesweepers which were trying to keep the Forth Bridge clear.

Barges, drifters and half a dozen luxury yachts, which had been commandeered by the R.A.F., were anchored in the estuary. From them, balloons were flown to deter low-level and dive-bombing attacks of boats which were in Rosyth dockyard for repair and refitting and for those ships anchored in the estuary awaiting the assembly of the convoys. The Forth Balloon Barrage consisted of fifty-one balloons; eleven on the water and the rest on land.

Under cover of darkness, when the convoy was complete, the ships would slide out of the estuary into the North Sea, en route to Scapa Flow in the Orkney Islands, the Home Fleet's main base. Convoys on the Atlantic run were prey to U-boat attacks. Convoys sailing to Russia not only ran the gauntlet of U-boats but were also subject to aerial bombardment and attacks from German destroyers based in Norway.

On watch on the yacht, *Ceol Mara,* Dad would hear the

throb of engines and see the great hulks slowly sliding away. From their vantage point in the estuary, Dad and his crew came to know the names of all the boats under their protection. They took a proprietary interest in their welfare and mourned the loss of those ships and men who did not return. Sometimes more than half of the ships in a convoy were sunk. The loss of life was appalling. The U-boats seemed invincible.

The yachts were not designed for the heavy equipment and winches which had to be set up on deck to fly a balloon. The balloons were massive; these leviathons were sixty-six feet long, contained nearly twenty thousand cubic feet of hydrogen gas and were suspended from cables up to 4,500 feet.

The yachts rode high in the water and rolled badly in heavy seas. Dad enjoyed his time aboard 'his' yacht, *Ceol Mara*, however. The crew's duties left a good deal of spare time which was devoted to playing cards, reading and fishing. Strictly against regulations Dad indulged his love of swimming most days, watched nervously by his crewmates. He would swim for an hour before returning to the cramped quarters of the yacht and the overpowering presence of the balloon.

Each yacht was manned by four balloon operators. The airmen took turns cooking. This became a distinct challenge when the boat was rolling. Eggs fished out of the scuppers after the stove suddenly tilted to a forty-five degree angle took on a distinctive flavour. There was an unspoken rule amongst the four men. No one ever criticized a chap's culinary efforts. If the offering did not make the grade, it was eaten in complete silence. If someone's cooking proved successful, lavish praise was heaped on the chef.

"This is great, Harry."

"Best bubble-and-squeak I've ever tasted."

No one enquired too closely into the secrets of any cook's cuisine.

When a fish was caught Dad's expertise was called upon. He gutted and filletted the fish, surrounded by screaming gulls as he threw the entrails overboard. In the summer months there were endless days of beautiful warm weather and fishing was a favourite occupation. But the balloon above and the ships on the water were a constant reminder that they were embroiled in a war.

Flying the balloons was not without its problems. Sometimes a balloon would mysteriously lose its hydrogen and the massive bulk of fabric would slowly descend and wrap itself over the boat deck. A brisk breeze was blowing one day when Dad was in the galley making one of his frequent sergeant's cups of tea - very sweet and strong enough to stand a spoon up in. He became aware of strange noises emanating from above. Cup in hand, he emerged on deck to find that his balloon had deflated and was in the process of draping itself neatly over the bow of a destroyer moored about one hundred and fifty feet away. He called his fellow crewman who was resting in his bunk.

"Jim, Jim, get your arse up here fast!"

They stood laughing, watching the last few folds of the balloon settling slowly, gracefully, like a dancer's skirts after a pirouette. The skipper of the destroyer, however, was not amused. Over a megaphone came an irate voice,

"What the hell do you think you're doing? Get this bloody balloon off my boat!"

He spoke as if they had dropped the balloon deliberately. Dad and Jim set to work immediately to retrieve the balloon but this proved to take some maneuvering.

"Wind the cable in, Jim. When it's taut we'll make our way

over to the destroyer."

As Jim cranked, Dad eased the yacht forward until they were alongside the destroyer. At this point the help of the destroyer's crew was needed. The skipper turned his back in disgust at the affront to his boat while the crew started to disentangle the balloon and heave it overboard. When the fabric was finally clear of the destroyer, Dad and Jim had the exhausting task of hauling the errant balloon out of the water, back aboard their yacht.

One night Dad came ashore with his buddy, Harry. Harry was dark-haired, short, tough, having a flattened nose acquired from one of many brawls in his native Liverpool. He was quick with his fists, good insurance against possible trouble. They tied up their boat at the pier and walked the three hundred yards to the pub. An assortment of men of all nationalities from the ships anchored in the estuary would gather at the Steamboat Tavern whenever they got a chance to come ashore: Australian, British, American. There were a few Norwegians and Poles: those who'd escaped before the Germans took over their countries. The free Poles, welcomed by the Scots, were based in Scotland.

A surge of sound erupted as they pushed the pub door open. Dialects, accents, idioms; Scots, Welsh, Cockney and Australian vernacular could be heard. If the Scotsman and Cockney found it difficult to understand each other, how on earth could a Norwegian or Pole comprehend any of it?

Along one wall was the bar with huge barrels stacked behind it. Behind the bar stood Mrs. Stark, an English lady, tall and well-proportioned. She was a friendly person with a good sense of humour, who made everyone feel welcome. On the opposite wall was a huge fireplace with a great coal fire burning. Seamen sat at tables playing dominoes and cards. Dad and Harry made their way to the bar, got their beers and then edged over to the side of the room to survey the scene. There was an air of tension. The convoy was almost complete. Each man knew this might be his last drink ashore before his ship sailed. It might be his last drink ever.

"Them's the chaps from *Narvik*."

Harry indicated a knot of men, in their long leather boots, at a table beside them, set apart by their language, Norwegian. They worked their way back to the bar for a refill.

"Where're the Sheilas?" an Aussie asked a Scotsman standing at the bar.

There was no response.

"Sheilas?"

Again, no answer.

"You know, birds."

Comprehension dawned.

"There'll be no gerrls here," in a voice of strong disapproval.

It was pitch dark as Harry and Dad left the pub. All light was blacked out. Not a glimmer showed as they walked carefully along the pier to where their boat was moored. Harry shone the torch onto the rungs as Dad made his way down the ladder.

"Here, Ed."

He threw the torch down for Dad to direct the beam for him. They started the engine, cast off and headed towards the yacht. A cry and a loud splash startled the quiet night. Not infrequently, sailors had drowned when they'd fallen off the pier in an intoxicated state.

"Another of them silly buggers," said Harry, "where is he?"

Dad directed the beam of light towards the cries as Harry steered the boat. They saw a man thrashing in the water. As he started to disappear below the surface they grabbed him and hauled him on board. Back at *Ceol Mara* they saw they had rescued a very young man who was barely alive. They stripped his clothes off, rubbed him down, wrapped him in blankets and gave him a hot drink.

"Tak, tak," he kept saying.

Olaf was from *Narvik* and he and his skipper were Norwegian. At first light Dad and Harry transported Olaf to his ship and watched while he climbed safely aboard. That afternoon a boat carrying two men appeared alongside *Ceol Mara*. The Norwegian skipper and a second man, each carrying a parcel, climbed aboard and were shown into the tiny cabin. The skipper unwrapped his parcel to disclose a bottle of Scotch.

"Tak for Olaf's life."

"Cheers."

"Skoal."

The Norwegians' understanding of English was extremely limited; Dad and his crew's knowledge of Norwegian was confined to the word 'skoal'. The first bottle was soon emptied. Their visitors would not allow the second one to be opened.

"For you, for you."

And away they went, back to *Narvik*.

LOWER LARGO

I'd discovered this little flat for rent in Lower Largo looking out over the Forth. It seemed just perfect. I could come there whenever I had leave and at low tide there was a marvellous beach for you girls to enjoy.

Lower Largo, where Dad found us a little flat, is situated in a bay on the north side of the Firth of Forth. The estuary is about ten miles wide at this point. The headland just east of the bay is open to the North Sea, stormy and cold and treacherous.

One day in early July we finally arrived at Leven, the nearest train station to Lower Largo. Air raid alerts delayed us several times en route and Dad had been hovering about at the station for hours. As we climbed down off the train, he came over and started hauling out first our bicycles, then our luggage, suitcase after suitcase, and lastly, Mother's sewing machine.

"Good heavens, Alice, what's all this?"

"All this," said Mother with some asperity, "is what I think three children and I will need for several months."

"I'll see if the stationmaster will keep the bicycles until tomorrow. We can come for them then."

Dad went off to negotiate this and then hailed the lone taxi. The driver looked at us, exhausted, dishevelled after the long journey, and then at the mound of luggage.

"I'll no manage in one go."

But in the end we all crammed in, the luggage was tied

onto the roof and we set off, the springs of the taxi screaming in protest all the way. Arrived at the flat we piled out and greeted our new home with delight.

It was a small flat, with a tiny kitchen, a fair-sized living room and two small bedrooms. We three girls just fitted into one of them. The flat was on the second floor, overlooking the estuary. The kitchen door opened onto a verandah which ran alongside the kitchen and living room. From the verandah a staircase extended to a grassed area below. Then a path led the way to the gate in the fence beyond which was the beach. It was too late to explore that night. We unpacked what we needed immediately and fell into bed.

Early next morning I jumped out of bed, ran into the kitchen, and flung open the door. It was almost daylight. I stood on the verandah and looked out at the water. The tide was high and the water was still. A wisp of cloud hugged the water, drifting slowly, dissipating. Then it was gone; the sky blazed blue; the day was wide awake. I was mesmerized by the silence, interrupted only by the screech of a lone gull and the lapping of the water. An occasional puff of white cloud floated by, high above. I gazed, entranced.

My eye travelled on and there were the ships of the convoy, anchored outside Methil just west of Largo Bay. There they sat, great behemoths, each one detached, yet belonging to the group. Convoys between Methil and Bergen, in Norway, had sailed from November, 1939, until April of 1940 when the Germans overran Norway. Many of the ships in the last convoy had been captured as they unloaded in Norwegian ports.

Lower Largo's sole claim to fame was that Alexander Selkirk, the original Robinson Crusoe, was born there. Whenever we walked down the street, the statue of Robinson

Crusoe, hand raised to shade his eyes, gazed down at us from his niche in the wall outside the cottage in which Selkirk had been born. Lower Largo boasted one shop, one hotel, The Crusoe, and one street. Main Road hugged the coastline. Along this road we walked when we needed more than the local shop offered, climbed up steep Serpentine Way, and ambled through the fields to Upper Largo where we bought our groceries. It was downhill all the way back.

Since there was less than a month of the summer term left, Mother and Dad decided that we should wait until September to start school. We had weeks of freedom in which to investigate the ever-changing riches cast up by the waves. Each day we waited impatiently for the tide to go out so that we could find new treasures. Rock pools were a source of unending delight. Every tide left behind a new configuration of pools with different inhabitants. On the balcony we each had a bucket of seawater populated by collections of unfortunate captives.

"You may keep your starfish and urchins in the bucket for a day," said Mother, "and then they must go back so that they don't die."

We made countless trips back and forth to the beach. Mother placed a bowl of water and a towel by the kitchen door.

"Wash your feet before you come in. I'm sick of sweeping sand out of this flat."

By the end of each day the bowl would be full of sand.

Mother loved winkles and I picked these off the rocks by the score for her to boil and eat. When they were cooked they had to be coaxed out of their shells with a pin. There was a hypnotic fascination to this activity; prying the winkles out and laying them one after another in a row on a platter; smelling the aroma of the ocean as they were ferreted out of their shells. I hated winkles myself and never ate them.

It was a perfect summer. Memories of the blitz faded from our minds. In the evenings Mother read stories to Jennifer while Clare and I played 'Snap', pretending not to listen. Then she tucked Jennifer into bed and sang to her the songs she had always sung to us - Old King Cole, Sing A Song Of Sixpence, and always at the end:

Now the day is over,
Night is drawing nigh,
Shadows of the evening
Steal across the sky.

Day after day blue skies prevailed; the sun shone on us. Dad joined us whenever he got leave. We swam with him, fished off the pier, threw balls, and ran wild on the beach. Dad was comfortable with girls; he'd had lots of practice with his sisters. Jennifer strove hard to keep up with us but sometimes she followed her own four-year-old agenda. One day she could not be found. Eventually we discovered her sitting at the end of the old stone pier, feet dangling, in her hand a stick to which she had tied a piece of string, 'fishing', as the waters swirled angrily about her.

Only the wireless intruded upon our world of delight. Every evening our landlady, whose husband was away at sea, came in for company. Mother would make a pot of tea before the news broadcast began and as they sipped their tea they listened to the news. Mrs. McGregor talked about Jock all the time.

"He's on the convoys. There's too many U-boats. So many ships go down. The lads don't stand a chance in that cold water. I'm feared for him."

Not until the Japanese attack on Pearl Harbour on December 7 did the United States enter the fray and Britain and the Commonwealth no longer fought alone. The war became global. The Allies were having a hard time of it. The Japanese were sweeping across the Pacific and Britain suffered heavy shipping losses.

But even the knowledge that Dad was stationed on a boat in the estuary at risk from attack by enemy planes could not mar our joy. We were just children; it was for the adults to agonize over the war.

September brought an end to this enchanted summer. School had to be faced. The shy, English girl was not well received at Leven High School.

"She's daft. She can't talk proper."

"Listen to her. She can't even say ff-our (four)."

The school wanted confirmation that I had passed the scholarship exam. By the time this was obtained and I was placed in the right form, three weeks of classes had passed. In the Latin lessons the automatic punishment for failing a test based on the previous night's homework assignment was three strokes of the strap on each hand. This was my first day in the class. When everyone who had failed the test lined up to be strapped, I was in the row. My hands trembled as the teacher stood in front of me. No one had ever struck me. Suddenly he said,

" You're noo, aren't ye?"

I nodded my head, incapable of speech.

"Sit ye doon then," and he moved on to the next victim.

I shared Dad's love of history, but here I discovered that the Scots' version of certain events was quite different from the accounts I had read in my history book at home. I was reading about the capture in 1346 of King David II of Scotland and the defeat of his army. Apparently he had been tricked by the English. Because of their dastardly actions he had been taken captive. I showed the text to Dad.

"This isn't right, Dad."

He read it and advised: "Write *their* version on your exam."

I was discovering that the writing of history is never disinterested and rarely objective.

Clare had her own problems at school. As she rode home on her bike each day she would be waylaid by several boys in her class who forced her off her bike and then let her tires down. After a few days of this, Clare, in her usual decisive way, took action. When everyone had left the classroom, she went to each boy's desk, took out his ruler, put them all in her pockets and set off for home. When she was accosted by the usual bullies, she jumped off her bike before they could grab her and laid about her to good effect with a fistful of rulers, whacking anything within reach. Her tormentors took off. Clare got back onto her bike, rode to the pier and threw the remains of the rulers into the ocean.

Next morning in Maths class the teacher said,

"Students, take out your pencils and rulers."

He never did get a satisfactory explanation as to why none of the boys could comply with his request.

We stayed in Lower Largo until January, 1942, when Dad was redeployed. On my last day at school, the music teacher, who'd discovered that I could sing, said,

"Perhaps you'd like to gie us a wee song before you go, Annette."

I stood up and without a moment's hesitation, sang;

There'll always be an England
While there's a country lane,
Wherever there's a cottage small
Beside a field of grain.
There'll always be an England

While there's a busy street;
Wherever there's a turning wheel
A million marching feet.
Red white and blue,
What does it mean to you?
Surely you're proud, shout it aloud....
There'll always be an England
And England shall be free,
If England means as much to you
As England means to me.

I sat down. There was silence. The girls all looked at Miss McFerrin for her reaction.

"Thank ye, Annette, and noo, Marcia, perhaps you'd gie us *oor* vairsion o' that."

Marcia stood up and sang;

There'll always be an England,
While Scotland's there to fight....

Here we were waging our own petty little wars while the great conflict raged just outside.

Lower Largo, 1941

Clare, Alice, Annette, Edward, Jennifer

LOSSIEMOUTH

I got to know some of the crews fairly well and became quite fond of these brave young men. When Xray disappeared it was a sad occasion. If a plane failed to return, flight mechanics were never given confirmation of its loss. We just formed our own conclusions as to what had happened.

The aerodromes at Lossiemouth and neighbouring Kinloss, in the north of Scotland, were opened in 1939. Initially, Lossiemouth was just a grass field but in 1942 proper runways were laid. Lossiemouth is located five miles north of Elgin. In this beautiful part of Scotland, the terrain is high and exposed to the elements. Winter weather is harsh, bitterly cold, and capricious. Bright clear days are interspersed with severe storms which sweep in from the North Sea.

Throughout the war, Lossiemouth was used by R.A.F. Bomber Command as a refuelling and maintenance stop and also for pilot training. Wellingtons, Ansons, and later, Lancaster Bombers were used for nighttime bomber training.

Dad was very familiar with the Wellington, having worked on it in the early days of the war when it was used on bombing raids. The Wellington had a lattice-like geodetic metal framework covered with a canvas skin. The 'dope' painted on the canvas shrunk and sealed it but also made it highly flammable. Nicknamed the Wimpy because of its portly contour, its cigar-shaped fuselage was distinctive. Like a beloved grandfather, it was elegant and substantial, trustworthy and reliable. It had proved capable of staying aloft even after sustaining a terrific amount of damage. Some made it back home in spite of having the turret, fin and rudder shot away. Even if the canvas covering had been burnt away, the Wellington was still capable of flying. It was held in great affection by pilots.

When first we met I felt afraid
You looked so cumbersome and staid
Standing quietly near the trees,
Shuddering gently in the breeze.
It seemed incredible to me
That you and I would ever see
Vast tracts of German territory.
Do you remember our first flight
Climbing steadily through the night?
We went to Bremen, I believe,
Or was it Kiel or Ludensheid?
But anyhow I could surmise
That in spite of your great size
You loved your element, the skies....

author unknown

The Wellingtons used for training at Lossiemouth were often quite elderly and had some odd idiosyncrasies. The accident rate on the Wellingtons was high. Bad weather, long training flights, and pilot fatigue and inexperience were contributing factors. In 1943, six Wellingtons with five or six men aboard each plane were lost. Rarely was any trace found of a missing plane. Occasionally an empty dinghy was picked up.

Accidents on the ground were not infrequent either. In 1943 and 1944, when Dad worked as a flight mechanic at Lossiemouth the aerodrome was crowded and space was at a premium. Planes were parked wingtip to wingtip. One of Dad's many duties was to guide the planes to their parking positions after landing. His friend, Jack, drove the jeep which he would position on the ground in front of the plane while Dad sat on the jeep's tailgate holding a light baton in each hand. As Dad began a slow rotation of his batons the pilot powered up his engines and followed the lights to his designated parking spot. One night a pilot used a little too much throttle and suddenly the propellers were uncomfortably close to the jeep.

Dad yelled to Jack,

"Put your foot on it. He's going to cut us into mincemeat!"

A quick glance over his shoulder showed Jack the huge bulk of the Wellington looming over them. He put his foot to the floor, almost throwing Dad off the back as the jeep took a sharp turn to the right, careened off the runway and came to a quick halt on rough ground. The pilot, with his guide having mysteriously disappeared, brought his plane to a stop. Somewhat shaken, Jack and Dad repositioned themselves ready to escort the pilot again. As time went on they became adept at avoiding being run down by these behemoths.

Sometimes disaster was narrowly averted. On one occasion a Lancaster bomber turned too sharply into his designated spot and bumped a Wellington. His props began chopping up the Wellington's wing but the pilot was alert enough to cut his fuel before an explosion could occur.

One morning at breakfast Dad heard an untoward screaming from the field where planes were parked. A mechanic was yelling,

"Bomb away! Run!"

Dad emerged from the canteen to see men sprinting away from the field. A 450 pound bomb had dropped to the ground during loading. Fortunately the safety pin for the fuse remained intact.

One of the first exercises a new pilot undertook was known as 'circuits and bumps'. A 'caravan' of seven or eight Wellingtons would be lined up, and one after the other take to the air, circle the drome, and then be brought in to land. Another phase of the training was called 'cross-country'. A plane would have enough fuel for about four hours' flying during which time crews of eight men were trained in navigation, use of guns and other skills.

The Wellington on which Dad worked, and for which he developed a great attachment, was called *X* for *Xray*. When *X* landed after a mission the crew had sometimes not had time to build up the air pressure in the cabin. To correct this problem Dad supplied bottles of compressed air to the cabin.

It was often bitterly cold as Dad walked around the plane checking the undercarriage, looking for anything which might compromise the plane's safety. In addition to ensuring that the plane was all right mechanically, Dad tried to keep the crew calm and happy. They had a difficult, dangerous job and while they were using *Xray,* he felt responsible for their safety. They were 'his' young men.

By means of the walkie-talkie he got to know some of the crews quite well by name and voice. He could not have recognized their faces. They flew by night. From among the last crew ever to fly in *Xray* he knew the tail gunner, Jimmy, by his New Zealand accent, and the pilot, a young Englishman, by his cultured Oxford voice.

Dad was getting a little tired of the pilot's continued requests:

"More air, please."

And then the tail gunner, apologetically,

"Sorry, Ed, we need more air."

One particular night this crew was out on a training flight. It was over four hours since they had left and a storm was blowing in. It was very cold. *Xray* was overdue and obviously running on reserve fuel. Dad and his crew had lit the main runway with flares and stood anxiously waiting, praying for *Xray's* return.

Finally they heard the sound of the plane's engines. But it didn't appear to be coming in to land. It circled, passed overhead, and circled again. Then came the pilot's voice,

"I can't make out the runway."

Visibility was worsening by the minute.

"I'll try for Kinloss."

There was a touch of panic in his voice. Then he cut off radio contact.

The stench of the flares was in their nostrils as Dad and his crew stood helplessly while the sound of the engines faded away. The pilot, obviously quite disorientated, was headed, not for Kinloss, but straight out over the ocean. They knew that they would not see *Xray* again. When the fuel ran out, the Wellington would plummet and those bright young men be plunged to their deaths in the frigid waters of the North Sea.

Printed by kind permission of Martin W. Bowman, author:

WELLINGTON The Geodetic Giant

WARTIME IN WEST WICKHAM

It was the lack of privacy in the Air Force which was hardest for me. I was thirty-four when the war began. Maybe it was easier if you were younger but I found it hard to take men en masse. I had not the slightest desire to be a Corporal or Sergeant. I just wanted to be left alone to do my job.

We were back in West Wickham and I began attending Beckenham Grammar School for Girls. Grandad had bought me a bicycle so that I could cycle the four miles to school each day. There was no money for train fare. The other pupils had started a term before, settled in, and made friends. I never did quite catch up or fit in.

It seemed I was to experience a similar problem to the one Dad had had at school. In Latin class one day, Miss Rose said,

"Translate this, Annette."

She pointed to the blackboard. I remained silent.

"Read the Latin words."

And then in exasperation,

"Read it!"

Still I said nothing. Tall, grey-haired, unsmiling, she had been terrorizing students year after year, ever since Mother had been in her class.

" Veni, vidi, vici...."

She stabbed at each word with her pointer.

"I can't see."

After an eye examination I was fitted with glasses and from then on was required to sit in the front row in all my classes. My days of skulking in the back row, reading a book under the desk, were over.

Wartime life dragged on. When our next-door neighbour, Mr. Moore, was on duty as an air raid warden, his wife came to our house. She did not like to be alone when there was an air raid. As soon as Mrs. Moore arrived Mother would make a pot of tea. A cup of tea was the panacea for everything. If you were tired or frightened, depressed or elated, too hot or too cold, a cup of sweet, milky tea was the remedy. As she sipped on her tea, Mrs. Moore would moan constantly,

"Oh dear, oh dear, oh dear."

Night after night we hovered over the wireless listening to the latest news of the war. Only when Mother went to bed was the wireless turned off.

Disaster followed disaster. Singapore fell to the Japanese; in North Africa, Rommel pushed the Eighth Army back; twenty-four out of thirty-nine convoy ships on their way to the U.S.S.R. were sunk; historic towns like Exeter, Bath and York were bombarded.

We had become inured to the intermittent whine of sirens heralding an air raid, although the intensity of the Blitz days had passed. The effects of the war became ever more apparent. Our surroundings became increasingly shabby. Nothing was painted; there was no paint to paint with. Fences fell down and stayed where they were; no one was there to fix them. I learned to patch the tires on my bike because Dad was not there to do it for me. Mother became adept with a hammer. We managed, as did everyone else.

Lawns were dug up and vegetables planted in their place. Mother had done this previously. Before her father had left to fight in France in World War I he had bought the eight-year-old a child's garden spade and fork and told her,

"You are to help your mother in the garden while I'm away."

When the milkman's horse and cart came by we looked to see if the horse had left any manure. If it had, someone raced out with a shovel, scooped up the steaming stuff and deposited it on the garden. One of our namesakes, Thomas Coppard of Brighton, had been fined in 1872 for 'taking away the town dung'. No doubt he had wanted it for his garden, too!

We became ingenious at stretching our food rations. Gelatine was mixed into the meagre allowance of butter. Neighbours swapped coupons. With three children, Mother had more tea coupons than we needed so she exchanged them for margarine to make cakes. We were introduced to powdered eggs, concentrated orange juice and a daily teaspoonful of cod-liver oil. The orange concentrate was a good substitute for the sweets we craved. Whenever Mother wasn't around we scooped it out of the can and ate it neat.

When a rare consignment of fresh oranges came in, we rushed to the shops, and queued up to get our share. The shopkeepers tried to be fair and allowed each shopper one pound - three or four oranges. Clare and I would go from one greengrocer to another and buy one pound of oranges at every shop. If we were lucky we came home with two dozen oranges between us. Then we each had a quarter of an orange every morning until they were consumed.

One morning when we were waiting in one of the interminable queues at a shop we heard the sound of a plane approaching. The woman in front of us turned round.

"What's that? There wasn't any siren."

We rushed outside. A lone German plane had somehow got through the defences and was flying very low, following the contour of the High Street. As it approached it swooped down and the gunner opened fire. People in the street threw themselves to the ground.

The shopkeeper stood at the door of his shop.

"Get back inside!" he shouted.

But the plane roared off, and everyone slowly got up. The excitement was over and no one had been hurt.

Dad was stationed at Scapa Flow in the Orkney Islands. Since it was so far north he was not able to take advantage of short leaves to come home. He'd have had to turn around and go back before he even arrived. We looked forward to his letters.

'These islands are beautiful; meadows and rolling green hills and red sandstone cliffs. The days are very long and the nights short, but this is reversed in winter. And I've heard tales of fearsome winter storms.'

Then he wrote to say that he was hoping to make it home soon for a week, but could not say exactly when to expect him. Several days later, early in the morning, there was a prolonged knocking at the front door. Then the pounding stopped. I opened the door to see Dad trying to find his key.

He looked up and said,

"Any danger of getting a cup of tea?"

I threw my arms round him and pulled him into the house. He had been travelling for the better part of two days and nights, standing most of the time. We put the kettle on and collected around him in the kitchen. When the teapot had been duly warmed and the tea made we sat down to have breakfast together.

"What are you doing now, Dad?"

"Still working as a mechanic. As an L.A.C. I'm given quite a bit of leeway in my work. I like the job."

"What's an L.A.C?"

"Stands for Leading Aircraftman. I didn't go to the right schools to be an officer. They wanted me to be a sergeant. Forget it. I'd make a poor fist of ordering a bunch of green recruits around and telling other people what to do."

When Dad had revived a little, we all went out for a walk. I was embarrassed about my developing breasts and walked with my arms wrapped around my body.

Dad spoke to me angrily,

"Put your shoulders back. Breathe deeply. Fill your lungs."

I could not remember him being angry with me before and didn't understand why he was so cross.

For a while, at the beginning of the war, theatres and cinemas had been ordered closed in expectation of a great air attack. But they soon reopened. The musical *Me and My Girl* was staged and on one of his leaves, Dad and Mother went to see it. After the show the whole cast sang and danced their way down Lambeth Walk as they sang:

You're a little Lambeth gel,
You're a little Lambeth belle,
You'll see 'em all
Doing the Lambeth Walk. Oi!

Papa contributed to the war effort by firewatching. Each evening he travelled to London where he spent the night aloft a tall office building, keeping watch for fires which might be started after incendiary-bomb attacks. Then he became ill with jaundice but for some time insisted on continuing with his job. Connie would go to the train station to meet him every morning and support him on the short walk home. Finally he had to give it up. When we went to see him I gazed in disbelief. He seemed to have shrunk. How could a person be so yellow? I did not know that he was dying of cancer of the liver.

Then I came down with measles. Aunt Constance agreed to have me stay with her so that Clare and Jennifer would not catch it. But no one expected that I would become as sick as I did, lying in a darkened room day after day. Aunt Constance had a difficult time of it going from one sick room to another but she was very kind to me.

Papa died soon after I returned home. Bobby was in the Army and he and Dad got leave for Papa's funeral.

"I haven't looked in the safe yet," said Aunt Constance. "Here's the key, Edward."

When Dad pulled out the contents of the safe, all that was to be found were losing tickets from the racetrack.

Sometimes Mother heard of someone who wanted to buy our clothing coupons. We couldn't afford new clothes, anyway. The allowance paid to a serviceman's wife was pitifully small and Mother had a hard time making ends meet.

"If you girls want any pocket money you'll have to earn it. I can't afford to give you any."

When Clare and I went to the newsagent to enquire about doing a paper route, we were welcomed. No one asked unnecessary questions about our ages. Mother decided that she could do with a little extra cash, too, and got herself a route. She, Clare and I left home at six o'clock each morning on our bikes to deliver papers. When we got to the shop the newsagent would have the route already made up, the house numbers written on each customer's choice of newspaper. There was still a good selection of newspapers from the popular *Daily Express* to the more liberal *Manchester Guardian.* On my route I delivered about seventy papers, walking up the path to the front door of each house, paper held in front of my face to catch the cobwebs. At the end of the week, when we were paid, I felt rich.

We kept it up until the flying bombs started. So many people fled the London area then, that it was difficult to know whether to leave a paper or not. When all the windows of a house were missing, it did not seem likely that anyone was still living there. The newsagent was very upset when we told her we were quitting.

"Who's going to deliver the papers now?"

During the school holidays we stayed with Grannie and Grandad. They lived near Otford, a village in the Kent countryside, about forty miles away. They had rented accommodation at a holiday camp which was shut down for the duration of the war. We took the train to Otford, with a couple of bikes aboard, and then walked to our grandparents' place, suitcases strapped to the carriers, bags dangling from the handlebars of the bikes.

Grannie and Grandad lived in a spacious bungalow, the main building of the camp. We had the entire camp to ourselves. Dotted about the extensive grounds were several cabins which we used for protracted games of hide-and-seek. In the swimming pool, empty except for a puddle of rain in the deep end, families of newts and frogs had taken up residence. We climbed down the steps and walked along the sloping floor of the pool to get a good look at them. Through fields of cowslips Clare and I ran, shouting to each other from vast distances, listening for the echoes. We picked masses of the tiny, delicate flowers and took them back home to give to Grannie.

Every evening Grandad made a little ceremony of winding up his grandfather clock. He opened the door, reached into the clock with his long, elegant fingers, and slowly pulled the chain until the weights were in position to run for the next twenty-four hours. He checked the time with his wristwatch, adjusted the big hands on the clock, if necessary, and closed the door. I never tired of watching this ritual.

Solid, comfortable, with warm, smiling brown eyes, Grandad had a shock of white hair and was very handsome. When he brushed his hair each morning he usually had an audience. On his dresser sat two silver hairbrushes. He took these up and used them alternately, never together, on either side of his head.

"Why do you have two brushes, Grandad?"

"So that when I disturb the little fellows on one side they never have a chance to settle on the other."

Grandad's shaving ritual fascinated us. From the cabinet he first took out his strop, cup of shaving cream with the brush inside, and straight razor. Then he hooked the end of the strop over the tap. He picked up the razor, opened it out and we watched as he sharpened the long shiny blade. Next the shaving brush was run under the tap and dipped into the mug of soap. After he'd lathered his face he took up the razor again. As he drew the blade over his face, gathering soap and beard before it in a grand sweep, we held our breath. Sometimes he nicked himself and there would be a collective gasp from his audience.

Grandad always had a pipe in his mouth and his moustache was stained yellow with nicotine. When his pipe needed refilling, he knocked out the ash and carefully packed it with tobacco leaves from a tin of his favourite Old Briar. A smell of pipe tobacco pervaded the house.

Gardening was Grandad's passion. Grannie enlisted our help to keep the cabbage butterflies at bay. Caterpillars were chomping their way through the vegetables.

"I'll pay you a farthing for every one you catch."

She supplied us with little nets and we set off in hot pursuit of cabbage butterflies. It was a sizzling summer day and the butterflies seemed dizzy with the heat. We caught scores. By the end of the day we were exhausted and Grannie had no money left. She rescinded her offer.

Grandad grew an immense variety of fruit - redcurrants, blackcurrants, raspberries, gooseberries, loganberries, strawberries. He had them all. In the autumn it was our job to pick the fruit and help Grannie make jam and pies. She loved us a lot and always gave us the benefit of the doubt. She was warm and soft and full of cuddles.

As he suffered from arthritis, Grandad could not walk very fast, but I enjoyed the slow saunter at his side every Sunday as we went down the hill to church. At the camp life went at a different pace and we could escape from the war for a while. We had glorious times there.

Amateur Athletic Association 20 mile race 1948

Edward Coppard (214)

FLYING BOMBS

We were hearing accounts of terrible damage inflicted by these diabolical things and I was worried sick. Then I discovered that you were all living right in their flight path, in the very shadow of a balloon.

At long last we began to hear some good news. Montgomery, the new British commander of the Eighth Army, was on his way to defeat Rommel; the Allies gained the upper hand over the U-boat menace; Italy surrendered. Finally, on June 6, 1944, the long awaited event happened. The Allies landed in Normandy. People began to hope that the interminable war might be drawing to a close but a new menace was about to be unleashed. Exactly one week after D-Day, the first flying bomb landed on London.

In the first week of the attacks there were ten thousand casualties. At one point a hundred bombs a day were arriving off the coast of Britain. People were too exhausted to cope with this new horror. They were affronted and terrified. Bomb blast from these one ton missiles caused tremendous damage and injury, sometimes over a radius of a quarter of a mile. We were more afraid of these than of any of the 'conventional' bombs we had endured. From their launching pads on the continent, they took off, headed for London. Where exactly they landed was completely arbitrary, determined by their altitude and by wind and weather conditions.

They looked innocuous enough, like toy planes up in the

sky - stubby, short-winged, spouting flames from the rear. But they were programmed robots. The fact that they had no pilot enhanced their horror. They were nicknamed buzz bombs, because of the snarling noise made by the roaring exhaust, or more popularly doodlebugs, because of the capricious way in which they apportioned death and destruction.

But as with everything else they had endured, people gradually adapted to the situation. As the bombs snorted their way overhead we ignored them until we heard the engine cut out. Our attention was then engaged, activity suspended. Where would it land? How long would it take? When we heard the explosion, we resumed what we had been doing.

My favourite place in our house where I would curl up with a book was on the settee in the living room. The settee rested under the bay window and on the wall at right angles to it stood the piano. One day I was in my usual spot while Mother was in the kitchen with Clare and Jennifer, making lunch. Mother had managed to get some fresh eggs, a rare treat, and promised us a special dish of scrambled eggs. Hearing the familiar snarl of a doodlebug, Clare jerked open the back door. She and Jennifer rushed out into the garden, watching the buzz bomb's progress until it was directly overhead.

I had heard the approach of the doodlebug, too. Then the sputtering stopped. A feeling of unease penetrated my absorption in the story of the first marathon race in ancient Greece. I got to my feet, eyes still on the book, and slowly moved towards the shelter in the other room. Mother was pushing Clare and Jennifer in the direction of the shelter while she shouted,

"Annette, come now. Now!"

An enormous explosion rocked the house. We ran outside to see where the missile had landed, the eggs forgotten. The bomb had exploded on a house at the end of the road, completely demolishing it. Everyone was in the street, looking first to see if anyone needed help. People stood silent, stunned, gazing at the dust rising from the obliterated house. The adjacent houses were badly damaged but miraculously, no one was hurt.

"The whole family left yesterday, you know," said a neighbour, "they'd all be dead now, for sure."

The garden of the house was familiar to us. When the family was away, we had scrumped apples from the tree behind the house. I gazed in disbelief. The apple tree was still standing.

We made our way back home and looked at the mess in the kitchen. Shards of glass lay over everything. Embedded in the scrambled eggs, fragments of glass glinted in the light.

"We can't eat those," said Mother angrily, and threw them away.

We walked slowly through the house to assess the extent of the damage. Most of the windows were shattered. Shards of glass were imbedded in the settee where I had been sitting and fragments of glass lay over all the piano keys. That afternoon we went around to different shops, scrounging pieces of cardboard to place over our missing windows.

Dad was stationed in Yorkshire near where an old family friend lived. He went for a visit.

"If it gets too bad, Alice and the children can come here, you know," said Joan.

"That's good of you."

Dad came home on leave. He had never seen a flying bomb. Clare and I went for a walk with him, one of us on either side, chatting to him, vying for his attention, proud of him in his smart uniform and cap. The air raid siren sounded and we turned for home. We heard the familiar sound of a doodlebug approaching and stopped. Looking up we saw the flames spouting out of it so Clare and I were not immediately worried and continued on our way. Suddenly Dad threw us to the ground and lay on top of us. We thought he'd gone mad.

"Dad, what are you doing? What are you doing?"

"The engine's still going. There's nothing to worry about!"

We were terribly embarrassed and scrambled hastily from under him, dusting ourselves off while Dad retrieved his cap that we had so admired from the gutter.

During the war years at Beckenham Grammar we had become used to continuing with our lessons in the shelters during air raids. When the siren sounded while we were in school we picked up our books and hurried down into the dismal, underground shelters. Sometimes the lantern was forgotten and we sang songs and told stories in the dark until the raid was over.

Raids seemed frequently to happen at dinnertime. Teachers would carry tureens of rabbit stew, with gravy dripping, across the playground to the shelters. The shelters often flooded and then all the students were marshalled at a run along the road to shelters near New Beckenham Station.

Doors were constantly blasted off the school building and once a nearby bomb shattered all the water tanks. Staff were called to the school at 7 a.m. and spent the day sloshing about in Wellington boots, sweeping streams of water down the stairs. It was the only day that the school was shut.

One day there had been an air raid just after dinner. When the all-clear sounded, instead of going back to class, students were dismissed. I set off to cycle home and then the siren sounded again. Aunt Constance lived near the school and I often dropped in to see her on my way home. But she was not there. As I was waiting for her to return I heard the well-known, menacing sound. There was a huge blast and the windows and doors blew in. My uniform was covered in dust and my ears hurt. I felt frightened and didn't want to be by myself. I walked slowly through the house to the front door which had been blown wide open. The lock was broken, but automatically I closed the door carefully behind me. Then I jumped onto my bike, and cycled off for home.

But my usual route was blocked. The buzz bomb which had damaged Aunt Constance's house had scored a direct hit on a canteen filled with people. A lot of workers were killed and injured. People were rushing around trying to help. Some of the victims were very badly hurt and some were obviously dead. A policeman was trying to clear the way for ambulances to get through.

"Take another way, Miss, this is no place for you."

For a while I was too horrified to move. People were placed on stretchers and taken away in the ambulances. I thought I was going to be sick. Wheeling my bike, I turned away. I felt too wobbly to ride. Finally I reached home. When I walked into the kitchen Mother looked at me.

"What's the matter? You're white as a sheet. Sit down, I'll make you a cup of tea." And she walked to the stove to put the kettle on.

"I'm not going to school any more."

Then reaction set in and I started crying. For nights I could not sleep. When I did manage to sleep, I had a recurring nightmare. In my dream I was lying in a street with a lot of other people around me. They were all dead but although I knew that *I* was alive, I could not move.

The attacks from buzz bombs escalated. We appeared to be right under the direct flight path of the missiles. And then in September came the V2s, long-range rockets, impossible to intercept because they climbed, after launching, to sixty miles. They were too high for the balloon barrage. They flew too fast for a plane to tip a wing and bring them down. As they flew faster than the speed of sound, there was absolutely no warning of their approach. These monsters were larger than the V1s and weighed fourteen tons. Wherever they landed they gouged small craters.

During the ten months of flying bomb attacks, nine thousand people were killed and twenty thousand injured in the Greater London area. In addition some six thousand houses were damaged or destroyed.

It was all too much, especially for Mother, solely responsible for the safety of three children. When another bomb exploded nearby, we departed for Otford. But as we were to discover, we had not escaped from danger.

Meantime, Dad, not sure what was happening to us, was worried. He got forty-eight hours compassionate leave and rushed home only to find an empty house. He pounded on the neighbour's door.

"Where are Alice and the children?"

"They've gone to her parents."

Dad hopped on to one of our bicycles and rode forty miles to find us. As he neared the camp, he saw a familiar sight. An anti-aircraft balloon was flying in the field next to my grandparents' place. He was horrified. When the flying bombs assaults began, a phalanx of balloons was set up in the flight path the bombs were programmed to follow. It was hoped that many of them could be brought down in the country before reaching London. The county of Kent came to be known as 'flying bomb alley'.

"You're right in the path of these things, Alice. This is no place for you and the children. It's more dangerous than West

Wickham. Send a telegram to Joan to say you're coming."

"What about Mother and Dad?" asked Alice.

But Grannie and Grandad refused to leave Otford.

We made our way back to West Wickham where Mother and Dad boarded over the windows and nailed up the front door. With our suitcases packed, we went early next morning to King's Cross Station to await the train for Leeds. Trains adhered to no schedule; no one knew when the train would arrive.

When we got to the station, the platform was packed solid with hundreds of people, mostly women and children, many of them homeless. Exhausted women sat on suitcases; babies cried; children screamed. The odd serviceman in uniform could be seen in the crowd. We waited and waited. Whenever a doodlebug was heard overhead, people quietened as everyone listened for the engine to cut out. When it stopped, no one spoke; even the babies stopped crying. Everyone was wondering whether it was going to fall on the station and kill us all. After each explosion there was a collective sigh of relief and talking gradually resumed.

After an eternity of time the train arrived. There was a tremendous cheer and we all clambered aboard. By common consent, seats were given to mothers with babies and to old people. We stood crammed together in the corridor all the way to Leeds. It was even worse to be standing there with the train stationary than it had been waiting on the platform. I had never felt so frightened. A buzz bomb was heard approaching. The sound stopped.

"Heads between your knees!" roared an Army sergeant to the people seated.

"Get down!" shouted Dad to everyone around as he pushed us to the floor.

Then the sergeant slammed open the compartment window and Dad yanked open the one directly opposite it in the corridor. The bomb fell near enough to shake the carriage but the anticipated blast was not felt. We scrambled to our feet. Jennifer put her hand in Dad's.

"When's the train going to start, Daddy?"

At long, long last the train started to roll. Someone started singing:

Pack up your troubles in your old kitbag,
And smile, smile, smile,
While you've a lucifer to light your fag,
Smile, boys, that's the style
What's the use of worrying,
It never was worth while, so
Pack up your troubles in your old kitbag,
And smile, smile, smile.

And everyone joined in.

WINTER IN YORKSHIRE

I was stationed nearby in Yorkshire while you were all staying with Joan, so Alice and I were able to get away together. She came to meet me and we had a wild weekend in Blackpool. That was the first time that Alice and I had been alone together for years.

Joan and her family had a big old house in Cookridge, near Leeds in Yorkshire. We arrived with our clothes, our bedding, our 'evacuation' blankets, and the faithful old hooped bicycle. From somewhere, Joan managed to find extra beds for us. It must have been very difficult for her and her husband, Harold, to have a woman and three children suddenly added to their household, but somehow they fitted us all in and did their best to make us feel welcome. Jennifer enjoyed having James and Anne, near her own age, to play with. Charles, the dog, however, did not appreciate the intrusion into his territory.

The house was a draughty place at the best of times. My overwhelming impression of our stay there was the pervasive cold of the house and how chilled I felt all the time. There were record low temperatures and huge snowfalls that last winter of the war and chronic shortages of fuel for domestic use.

Getting from the house to the main road in order to board the bus for school, when it was running, was a major problem. There were only two pairs of large Wellington boots in the house and there were no boots to be had in any shop.

Each morning Mother put on one pair, while I stepped into the other and as I carried my own shoes, we made our way through the drifts to the road. There, hanging onto Mother for support, I changed from the boots to my own shoes, ready to board the bus. Carrying the relinquished boots, Mother then went back to the house and followed the same procedure with Clare.

After that it was the turn of the younger children to be escorted to the primary school at the top of the hill. Fortunately James and Anne each had their own boots but Jennifer had to wear one of the large pairs. For a child with small feet it required a strange sliding, thrusting motion, toes rammed against the end of the boot, to move each foot forward. If she tried to go too fast she would fall flat on her face. If she lifted her foot off the ground, she risked stepping right out of the boot. When we came back after school, Mother or Joan would be waiting for us, boots in hand, to escort us back to the house.

One weekend James and Jennifer set off up the hill, each in a pair of boots approximately the right size. They joined some classmates and built an enormous snowman.

"Let's roll him down the hill."

It seemed impossible to move the snowman. In the children's efforts to mobilize him, his head became detached. It rolled beautifully, gathering speed as it travelled down the hill, getting bigger and bigger. They raced after it. At the bottom of the hill the gigantic ball came to rest, towering over the children as they stood beside it.

Joan was a tall, big-boned woman with large hands and feet. She was loud; her voice filled the house. She was good-natured. She was eccentric. I came upon her one night in the bathroom. As in most English bathrooms of that time there was no heat of any kind.

"You can come in if you want to. I'll just be a minute."

I sat on the edge of the bath, shivering, my 'evacuation' blanket wrapped around me. The blanket, five years after it had been issued, was decidedly the worse for wear. Its value in terms of warmth was questionable but I still found it comforting. Joan was washing her face in the sink.

"Is it often as cold as this in Yorkshire?"

"It's always cold in this house. You'll get used to it."

Having dried her face, she then bent down, took the sock off her left foot, dipped her foot into the sink and washed it. She put her foot to the ground and dried it. I waited, expecting her to repeat the procedure with her right foot. But she let out the water from the sink, picked up her sock, the towel she had been using, and walked towards the door.

"It's too cold. I'll wash the other foot tomorrow."

Getting ready to go to bed was a considerable undertaking. An hour or so before bedtime you heated water to fill the brownstone hot water bottle and placed it in the bed with your pyjamas, a woolly jacket and bedsocks wrapped around it. A major decision had to be made as to which small section of the bed was to be made warm. Since my feet were always colder than any other part of my body, I usually opted to place the bottle at the end of the bed. After the absolute minimum of washing, you ran into the bedroom, tore off your clothes and put your pyjamas, bedsocks and jacket on as fast as possible. Next, you put your clothes carefully between the top blanket and the eiderdown to ensure that in the morning your clothes would not feel damp. Then you dived into bed. I learned to get through this procedure very quickly.

The cold was debilitating and I never did become acclimatized to it. As soon as I got home from school each day I wrapped my blanket around me and tried to get the chair nearest the fireplace in the living room, before any of the other children. This was Harold's chair and when he came home I relinquished it. But if Charles, Harold's whippet, were ensconced, I had no compunction in turfing him out. Charles and I were constantly in conflict although it was a war waged in silence. In keeping with all the other members of the family, he had a royal name, of course. As soon as I entered the room, if he were not already there, Charles immediately jumped up on the chair and hunkered down, ready to defend his territory.

We all hated the dog, but since he was a great favourite of the family and we were guests in their house, we could not express our feelings. I did not think he was a 'proper' dog at all. He was smooth and angular, very self-contained, silent and sly. We found it thoroughly objectionable that he was allowed to sit on the furniture. When he came in from outside he immediately jumped onto the nearest chair and began turning around and around, rubbing himself against the fabric until he was satisfied he'd found the most comfortable spot.

Dad was stationed not too far away and so we saw a little more of him than we had during the previous few years. When Dad got a forty-eight hour pass, he and Mother decided to go for a weekend together to Blackpool. Mother returned in a good mood. She was giggling to herself.

"What are you laughing at?" we asked.

"I was thinking of the landlady at the boarding house where we stayed. She was a real old battleaxe. She locked the doors at ten p.m. but she wouldn't give us a key. When Dad and I came back from the pictures a little after ten we couldn't get in."

"What did you do?'

"We walked to the back of the house and luckily found the

kitchen window open. So I had to balance on your father's shoulders and climb in. I landed with a big clatter amongst a pile of dishes on the counter."

"Did you wake up the landlady?"

"No. I waited a few minutes to see if anyone had heard before I crept to the back door to let your father in. Then we tiptoed upstairs to our room."

Mother and Joan wanted to have a good celebration at Christmas. Mother managed to save enough money to buy some material and made dresses for herself, Joan and all the girls. Clare and I braved the snowdrifts, some as tall as the tops of the trees, to collect branches of holly which we brought back to the house for decoration. Jennifer, James and Anne cut strips of coloured paper and made paste of flour and water to make ornaments for the tree. It was impossible to get a turkey but Joan managed to acquire a goose. Dad got leave unexpectedly and made a great job of carving. On Christmas morning there was one present for each child under the tree and we shivered for a day while we proudly wore our new dresses. It was a great Christmas.

And then Mother and Joan had a big row and we left Joan's. The row was over the dog. The adults had been invited to a party on New Year's Eve and Mother was sitting in the living room, waiting for Joan.

"I'm ready," said Joan, entering the room.

Clare and I admired their dresses as they twirled around, showing off.

"Mother, you've got a black mark at the back of your dress."

Mother held out her dress and turned her head until she could see the streak of mud.

"It's that damned dog. He's disgusting. Why do you let

him sit on the furniture!"

All her frustrations spilled out; everything she had kept bottled up. She did not go to the party.

Mother made arrangements for Clare and me to stay elsewhere. Clare went to live with people in the local 'big house' where she had a great time. I resided with Mrs. Harman, who needed a babysitter for her small son. Mother, taking Jennifer with her, went to stay with her father's sister in Devonshire, promising to send for Clare and me as soon as possible. When I came down for breakfast the first morning at Mrs. Harman's house, she led me over to the kitchen table.

"Here's your rations for the week," she said, pointing to a tiny dish of jam, a small pot of sugar and a pat of butter. "Ours are separate from yours."

I was humiliated. Did she think I was going to eat more than my share? She had certainly let me know I wasn't considered part of the family. At her house I was lonely and miserable and felt quite abandoned. I was longing to get back home.

Finally we did, one day in early March of 1945, when the flying bomb menace had almost ended. Mother, with Jennifer in tow, just appeared at the house where I was living. I had never been so glad to see them.

"Pack your things; we're going home."

Late in the evening we took a train back to London, dozing in fits and starts throughout the night. I fell asleep, with my cheek resting on a bar of chocolate on the table in front of me. By the time we arrived at King's Cross the chocolate was a melted mess. It was the early hours of the morning and we had a problem. Buses and tube trains were not yet running and there were no taxis either. We needed to get to Charing Cross for a train to West Wickham. So we walked. It was a very long way.

Everything was strangely quiet and pitch dark because of the blackout. Around a window an occasional chink of light showed. A car with dimmed lights passed us.

"Are you sure we're going the right way, Mother?"

"Oh yes," she replied, with a confidence she did not feel.

At each crossroad she stopped to get her bearings and then on we went. I was wheeling the big old bike while the others balanced all our paraphernalia on it as best they could. We must have looked a strange sight. A policeman on patrol was the only person we saw. He stopped and asked,

"Are you all right, Ma'am?"

"Oh, yes, thank you."

As we approached Covent Garden the market was beginning to come alive. We were nearly at Charing Cross. When we finally arrived home, absolutely exhausted, it was to find that the boiler had burst and the floors were awash. But it was so good to be back that I didn't care.

POLYTECHNIC HARRIERS

MARATHON RACE

INCORPORATING A.A.A. CHAMPIONSHIP, 1948.

26 Miles, 385 Yards. **19th July, 1948**

WINDSOR CASTLE TO CHISWICK STADIUM · LONDON

By the Gracious Permission of H.M. KING GEORGE VI. this race was started in The Quadrangle of Windsor Castle

This is to Certify *that, in the above race, started by Her Majesty Queen Elizabeth, in the Presence of H.M. King George Sixth.*

Mr. E. A. Coppard.

Club Kent A. C.

Finished 44th *Position.*

Time: 3 *Hrs.* ___ *Mins.* ___ *Secs.*

Signed [illegible] *Signed* [illegible]

DEMOBILIZATION

I couldn't believe the way in which some people carried on when it was all over. As for me, I was just immensely relieved to be going home. The war took six years out of my life. Six years with no money and nothing to show for it at the end.

Towards the end of the war, everyone had had more than enough of life in the services. Along with five million other servicemen and women, Dad was longing to be demobilized and get back to his family and civilian life. He was tired of the regimentation, the lack of privacy, and never having any money. Priority for release was determined by age and length of service. Dad had been in the Air Force for six long years so he was one of the first scheduled to be demobbed.

Tension was high and tempers were short. Fred, a big man, was rather a bully. People avoided him whenever possible. At mealtimes Dad usually sat with his friend, Matthew. One day at breakfast in the canteen Dad was ahead of Fred in the line. Dad had picked up his toast and then realized that he'd forgotten the marmalade. He took a step back.

"Excuse me," he said, and reached for the marmalade.

"Get out of my way."

Fred shoved Dad aside. Inwardly fuming, Dad waited while Fred moved ahead. Then he got his marmalade and returned to sit beside Matthew who was already seated at the table.

"Why did you let him push you around? What's the matter with you? You know, Ed, you're a chicken-shit bugger. You're so yellow there's a big streak about a foot wide running right down your back. You make me sick to my stomach. Don't class me as your friend any more. I don't want to know you."

While he listened to this harangue, Dad watched Fred finish his meal. When Fred got up and went to the trough to wash his eating irons he walked over and stood beside him.

"You made me look a right Charlie back there, didn't you?"

"Did you get your marmalade?" sneered Fred, as he turned to face him.

With a swift punch, Dad knocked him down. Fred's eating irons clattered to the floor as he fell. He got up and raised his fists. Dad struck him to the floor again. Fred staggered to his feet and Dad knocked him down a third time. Then he walked away and sat down beside Matthew. Only in the boxing ring had he ever struck anyone before. The interested group of spectators who had gathered to watch the entertainment were disappointed that the action seemed to have fizzled out. Surrounded by his supporters Fred left the canteen.

"What've you done? Now you're for it," was Matthew's helpful comment.

"The anger's gone out of me now," said Dad, "I feel sorry and really stupid."

He couldn't finish his meal.

In the hush which had fallen over the canteen, heavy footsteps were heard approaching. At the door appeared a military policeman.

"Don't move, anybody. Stay just where you are."

There was a second policeman guarding the other door. Fred came in, pointed at Dad and said,

"That's him."

The policeman spoke to Dad.

"Did you strike this airman?"

"I've never seen him before in my life."

"Report to the guardroom in half an hour."

Dad started stewing about it; here he was, due to be demobbed in a short while, and he'd struck a fellow airman. There were fifty or more witnesses to what he had done. He could go to the glasshouse for ninety days.

Later, in the guardroom, the flight sergeant took notes while Fred told his story of a totally unprovoked attack. Then Dad spoke.

"He did provoke me, sir," and gave his version of the encounter.

Fred was asked to leave.

"I've looked at your service record, Coppard. I see you have never been in any trouble. What group are you?"

"Group 12, Flight."

"Then you could be out very soon. Or if the old man drops the axe it could be ninety days for you. Come back in an hour. I'll see what I can do for you."

When Dad reported back, the flight sergeant said,

"You're lucky, Coppard. Your six years' good record got you off the hook. Get out of here and behave yourself."

"Thanks, Flight!"

While waiting for demobilization, Dad was stationed at a camp in the grounds of a large estate. The house and grounds, which had been commandeered by the R.A.F., were surrounded by a great ditch filled with water. There wasn't much to do and the officers tried to keep the men fit. The sergeant devised an exercise in which each man, carrying a pack and rifle, was required to cross the ditch by means of a pole greased with dirty used oil. No one made it across.

Everyone fell through the layer of thick, green scum into the water below.

Observing this fiasco Dad decided he would have no part of it. He viewed it as a singularly useless activity. In anticipation of his release, Dad had already begun to distance himself from the R.A.F. He followed the line of men approaching the ditch but when it was his turn to cross he quickly veered left and ran off, parallel with the ditch.

"Come back, that man, come back."

Dad had figured correctly that the sergeant wouldn't leave the other men to come after him. He kept running as the sergeant's shouts receded, and rejoined the group when that absurd activity was over.

That night, in company with several others, Dad sneaked out of the camp. They opened the vents to the ditch and by morning all the water had drained out. The sergeant could do nothing, short of charging fifty men. There were no more gymnastics over ditches.

When an army unit passed through the camp one day a huge row ensued. The men had been out on an exercise and returned to camp soaking wet, cold and exhausted. The transportation arranged for them was nowhere in sight. They were thoroughly disgusted.

"Let's get warmed up, anyway," said Jim, a tall lanky man, as he grabbed an empty drum.

He goaded the others into action.

"Get some wood and paper, you useless buggers."

They scattered in all directions. Jim went off in search of an unattended can of petrol. His mission was successful and they all converged with paper and assorted pieces of wood which were thrown into the drum, liberally sprinkled with petrol, and ignited. They stood around the fire, thawing themselves out. Sam and John were the most productive.

They arrived with an armful each of thin slats about two feet long. The slats burned beautifully, being clean and dry.

"Where d'you get these?" demanded Jim, but Sam and John were evasive in their answers. By the time the fire burned out, the trucks had arrived and the army blokes, a little dryer and warmer, went on their way.

Then the chaps in Dad's hut returned and, as usual, after the day's exertions, threw themselves on their beds.

"What the hell?"

One after the other the mattresses sagged and collapsed and their occupants crashed to the floor. An investigation revealed that each cot had only two slats remaining, barely enough to hold the mattress in place when there was no one on it. There was universal consternation.

"Who did this?"

"Is this someone's idea of a joke?"

A fist fight seemed about to erupt when Matthew cried out,

"It's them army blokes! They had that big fire outside!"

It was no good going after the culprits. Their trucks were long gone, and everyone's immediate concern was how they were going to sleep that night. The only thing to do was to place the flimsy mattresses on the floor and make the best of it. The following morning, the sergeant had to deal with the problem of the demolished beds.

When Ted had died in 1943, Dad thought that he would be able to take over his father's shop at the end of the war. But the premises were bombed, and that was no longer an option. He did not relish the idea of working for someone else after being his own boss, and agonized over what he was going to do to earn a living. When he heard that there was a course being offered to servicemen which would qualify him as a Physical Education instructor, he was elated. He spoke to his flight sergeant.

"I'd like to take the P.E. instructors' course, Sir."

"How old are you, Coppard?"

"Forty, Sir."

"You're a bit long in the tooth, Coppard. It's a difficult course."

"I did a lot of swimming and running before the war, Sir, and I've swum in several R.A.F. swimming galas. I like working with young people. I think I could handle it."

"Very well. I'll put your name forward. Good luck."

"Thanks very much, Flight."

The course was tough. Most of the men were more than ten years younger than Dad but he held his own. Then in the last week of the course, while doing a forward roll over a high horse, he broke his collarbone, and had to drop out. Dad was devastated. The door through which he had hoped to walk to a new and brighter future slammed shut. He was too diffident to plead his cause and the course was not repeated. He spent a miserable few inactive weeks waiting for his collarbone to mend. It was back to filling in time.

The big day finally came when everyone was drawn up on the parade ground and names were read out. For those like Dad who had been in from the very beginning, their stint in the R.A.F. was over. Others were being sent on to other dromes and departments of the R.A.F. before eventual demobilization.

Some men and women had worked together for several years and formed liaisons which now had to be severed. The chrysalis was broken. Emerging from their cocoon they faced reality and would have to try and pick up the pieces of their former lives. As names were read out for the deployments they wept and hugged each other.

"Write to me, Johnny."

"I'll come and see you, Angela."

Dad was astounded at their public expression of emotion. Women would go back to their homes to await their husbands' return from overseas. Men would go back to their wives in towns and villages all over the British Isles. Women whose husbands had been killed had no such reunion to anticipate. The future was uncertain.

After six years of war there was pain as well as joy.

Picture reproduced by kind permission of Kingston Athletic Club and Polytechnic Harriers

King George VI and Queen Elizabeth chatting with officials and contestants in Quadrangle of Windsor Castle prior to Her Majesty starting marathon race of 1948

(Dad standing behind official facing Queen Elizabeth)

AFTER THE WAR

The Elephant and Castle had been demolished. It wasn't only the bomb damage everywhere, although that was bad enough. But the heart of it was gone. The people were gone. The old Cockneys with their love of life were gone. I thought of Gilbert Parker's words: 'And the old days never will come again.'

The war in Europe was over. VE Day was May 8, 1945. Just two months later, on July 25, the Labour Party swept into power with Clement Attlee as prime minister. Grandad was stunned. He was in shock. He revered Churchill.

"How could they do this to him?" he lamented.

He was depressed for days. But whereas people respected Churchill for his leadership during the war, they were looking for a better life after the war, with employment for everyone and houses of their own. They saw the Labour Party as the means to achieve their aspirations.

Dad was demobilized on August 14, 1945, the same day that Japan surrendered. It was six years almost to the day after he had joined up. He went to the distributing centre where he collected his 'demob' outfit. After his measurements were taken he proceeded to the stores to be issued with his clothes.

Every serviceman was given a suit, a shirt, a pair of shoes, socks and underwear, and a hat. A cardboard box was furnished in which to carry the clothes. Service personnel were also given a gratuity, the amount determined by rank and length of service, to tide them over until they got a job. That evening Dad arrived unexpectedly at the door, carrying his cardboard box, back home for good.

"Well, that's it. It's all over. I could do with a cup of tea, lass."

Next day was VJ Day. Clare and I wanted to go up to London that evening to join the crowds celebrating in the streets.

"I'd better come with you," said Dad. "It'll probably be a bit wild."

Clare and I wore our best skirts and blouses, Dad donned his grey 'demob' suit, striped shirt and tie and off we went. The atmosphere in Piccadilly Circus was electric; everyone was singing and laughing. We watched as they danced along. People were pressed so tightly together that we had little control over our movements.

Clare and I clung to Dad, one on either side. Gradually we worked our way out towards the periphery of the crowd and made our way on to Regent Street. Pairs of women, GIs and girls, were dancing in the middle of the street. Someone had a trombone and from the sidelines we joined in as everyone sang the old favourite songs of the war years:

There'll be bluebirds over the white cliffs of Dover,
Tomorrow, just you wait and see.
There'll be love and laughter and peace ever after,
Tomorrow, when the world is free.

And then:

When the lights go on again all over the world
And the boys are home again all over the world....

It was good to have Dad back home. Our lives settled into

a routine with Dad a permanent part of it instead of being a 'visitor' on leave. As far as we girls were concerned he moved back very easily into our ménage which Mother had run by herself for six years. We were comfortable with Dad; he accepted us as we were; made no demands. Before long we took him very much for granted.

But post-war England was very depressing. The euphoria generated by VE Day and then VJ Day soon dissipated. Food rationing was still in force and everything was in short supply. It was all so rundown, dismal and drab; piles of rubble and abandoned buildings everywhere. In London alone, seven hundred thousand houses needed bomb damage repair. People were fed up, tired of deprivation and the continuing austerity, exhausted after six years of war. But it was not to get any better for a very long time.

We had heard accounts on the wireless of the hideous conditions Allied troops discovered as the Nazi death camps were liberated. When Clare and I went to our local picture house to see a newsreel about Belsen concentration camp, an usherette said to us,

"Are you sure you want to go in, dearies? You'll maybe find it too much."

The pictures jerked across the screen, human beings with sticks for arms and legs, like puppets in slow motion. Some of them were unable to walk, many of them only hours from death. Clare and I clutched each other's hands. I closed my eyes and then was compelled to look again at the screen. We saw piles of bodies that had been people. They looked like huge stacks of firewood.

Afterwards, as we walked out of the theatre, no one spoke. No one looked at anyone else. The horror of it haunted me for weeks. I could not get the images out of my mind. I wished I had never seen them.

Dad went up to London to see what had happened to Draper Street. Over half of the buildings in the Elephant and Castle area had been destroyed or badly damaged in the Blitz. Standing in the ruins of the street, Dad surveyed the rubble that had been his father's shop. The shop in Loampit Vale was gone and the one in Draper Street too. He couldn't renew a license for non-existent premises.

Ted had always had a stall outside his shop to sell his off-cuts. He'd employed a young person who wanted to get into the business. So Dad got a trader's license, set up a street stall and sold fish alongside other vendors. This was what he was reduced to.

"I took a walk around the Elephant today," Dad told us shortly after he set up his stall. "There's nothing left. And not too many customers. They're talking about a massive reconstruction of the whole area. I don't know how long the stall will last."

He was worried.

Dad was up very early in the mornings; he stoked the range by which the water was heated and then was off for Billingsgate Market to buy his fish for the day before going to his stall in Draper Street. Each evening he returned home with the Evening News tucked under one arm and a bag with fish or meat for the evening meal hanging from the other.

Meantime, he began proceedings to get compensation for the loss of his father's property. But this was never forthcoming.

Shortly after opening the stall Dad got a fish-bone stuck in his finger. It became infected. His finger swelled alarmingly and then telltale streaks began creeping up his arm. Dad was running a fever and we were concerned for him. He closed the stall and went to see the doctor. In 1945 penicillin was still not available to the civilian population in doctors' offices. Every day for two weeks Dad travelled by train to a London hospital to get a penicillin injection.

"Which side today?" the nurse would ask before plunging a needle into the designated buttock.

Slowly the red streaks subsided and Dad's arm was saved.

Later in the year, because of recurring sinus infections, I went into hospital to have my tonsils and adenoids removed. What should have been a routine procedure turned into a nightmare. At the end of a week during which I had not been able to swallow anything other than liquids and was not able even to talk, the hospital discharged me. At home that evening I started to cry I felt so awful. Suddenly I choked and then coughed up the cubed gauze swab which the surgeon had left in me. The swab smelt foul. Of course no doctor had come very close to examine me.

Next morning Mother went round to the doctor's surgery to ask him to come and see me. When he arrived at our house later in the day, he decided the situation called for extra rations for me, and also penicillin which by that time he was able to dispense. So I, too, was an early recipient of the wonder drug.

Immediately after the surrender of Japan in August, Lend-Lease had been abruptly terminated by President Truman. Lend-Lease, which Churchill had negotiated with the United States in 1941, had allowed Britain to defer payments for weapons, materials and food received. Now goods would have to be paid for straight away. Britain was virtually bankrupt and although the immediate crisis was staved off by a hurriedly negotiated loan, Britain's economic plight worsened.

In early 1946, food rations were cut to below wartime

levels and in May, bread was rationed for the first time. Queues for food were even longer than they had been during the war. Very little of anything was available for home consumption. Thousands of families still had no home of their own.

The fish stall did very well for a while although Dad felt his loss of status very keenly. Food shortages continued, and rations were to be cut even further, but we ate royally. Dad traded fish with other vendors and came home every night with meat, fish, fruit and vegetables. He brought his choice eels which only he and Clare liked.

"Daughter, I've got some eels for you."

She would watch while he cut them up and placed them in a very large saucepan to boil. Then they were put in a bowl and left to cool off. Sometimes when Dad wanted a late-night snack of this delicacy, the bowl of eels would be nearly empty. He just laughed, pleased that she shared the same taste.

"You don't take any of the ends either, do you, or the jelly, just the thick bits?"

We savoured our first bananas since the war began.

"Are they good, Daddy?" asked Jennifer.

Dad looked at her.

"Of course, you won't remember when you last had one. You were only two when the war began."

Poultry was very hard to come by but Dad occasionally came home with a chicken or turkey, complete with feathers and feet. He plucked and cleaned the fowl, feathers flying, while Sukey, our little black and tan terrier, ran madly around the kitchen in circles chasing them. It was bedlam. It was fun. He then draped the bird's feet over the top of the back door, closed the door and yanked on the bird. This procedure pulled the sinews out of the legs and the red feet, still attached, would be dangling on the other side of the door. He opened the door, took down the bird, cut off its feet, and completed dressing the fowl ready for Mother to cook. Lastly, he cleaned the top of the door.

At grammar school I was preparing to write the General Schools Examination in the spring of 1946, and trying to fill in the gaps left from the fractured schooling of the war years. I hoped to be able to go to college and become a teacher, so I needed to pass these exams. In geography I had studied Australia five times in five different classes, but not much else. It didn't seem possible that I could make up the lost ground.

Shakespeare's *Henry V* was on the curriculum that year for English Literature, and special daytime showings of Laurence Olivier's epic film of the play were arranged for schools. It was quite an experience to be in a huge theatre filled entirely with fifteen and sixteen year olds. Each time a hail of arrows from the English archers checked the advance of the French cavalry, a great cheer arose from all the boys in the audience. My friends and I fell instantly in love with Laurence Olivier but our reactions were more restrained.

After the film we claimed ownership of Olivier's many attributes:

"He's so handsome."

"Did you see how his eyes flashed?"

"That dimple in his chin!"

"And his voice!"

For days we all went around declaiming the famous speech:

Once more into the breach, dear friends, once more,
Or close the wall up with our English dead…
The game's afoot :

Follow your spirit; and upon this charge
Cry, "God for Harry, England, and Saint George!"

Each year the school put on a Gilbert and Sullivan operetta and I loved participating in these productions as a member of the choir. In my last year at school, I approached Miss Wiseman, the music teacher.

"Do you think I could ever be good enough to have a solo part?"

"Come after school tomorrow and let's see what you can do," she said.

She gave me a lead part and spent a lot of time working with me. At home I practised by the hour. Nancy Wiseman believed in me and finally I began to believe in myself. After the first performance, the geography teacher who had despaired of me came up and said,

"I didn't know you had it in you to do that, Annette. Congratulations."

Grannie and Grandad were with us for Christmas of 1946. This was the first celebration we had had all together since before the war began. Dad's gifts on Christmas Day were without question the most prized. For Mother he had perfume, and for Clare and me our very first pairs of nylons, all acquired on the black market.

DIFFICULT TIMES

I hated those jobs, being a barrow boy - I did that for more than five years - and working in that god-awful factory. But I had to earn a living. The only thing that kept me going was my running. When I was running I could forget all my problems.

January 1947 was the coldest winter recorded since 1880. Fuel shortages caused a great deal of hardship. Industries closed down for lack of power and for several hours each day, people in their homes were not allowed to turn on electric heaters. There were frequent power cuts. Austerities continued. Women were even exhorted to ignore Christian Dior's 'New Look' with longer skirts, in order to save cloth.

There were, however, a few bright spots in the pervading gloom. In August the Edinburgh Festival was inaugurated, bringing distinguished artists from over two hundred countries, and in November, people celebrated for a day with the marriage of Princess Elizabeth and Prince Philip. We grabbed the *Evening News* from Dad when he came home and pored over the pictures of the royal couple. Their wedding was seen as a symbol of better times for everyone.

Grannie and Grandad had bought a house in Cranbrook in Kent, near to their son, Edwin. He and his family lived on a farm and Edwin was also a volunteer ambulance driver. Most weekends Mother, Clare or I would go there to help Grannie and Grandad do their chores and get their groceries.

They tried different ways to stretch the meagre food rations.

"I hear they have some whale meat today," said Grannie, as I was leaving for the shops. "That's not rationed. Get some for us."

I had prepared what we thought would be a special treat. On the plates the whale meat looked inviting, like steaks. We anticipated a marvellous meal. But the first bite was enough. Suddenly it seemed as if you had a mouthful of wartime cod-liver oil.

One wintry weekend Clare went to visit Grannie and Grandad. The roads were icy and there was thick fog. She was travelling on the upper deck of a bus which hit an articulated lorry head-on. Clare was thrown forward into the handrail in front of her, was rendered unconscious and slid to the floor. Her front teeth had been knocked out and were sticking in the roof of her mouth. When the police came upstairs to see if anyone needed help no one saw her.

People were lined up on the roadside, waiting for ambulances to take them to hospital. Clare regained consciousness, got to her feet and walked towards the stairs. But the bus was lying at an angle, she lost her footing and fell right down the stairwell, injuring her back. She landed in a snowdrift at the feet of a policeman.

"Where on earth did you come from?"

"Down from the sky, of course."

'A stupid question deserves a silly answer,' thought Clare.

The policeman helped her to the side of the road where she sat in the freezing cold alongside a woman with pieces of glass sticking out of her side and the lorry driver whose legs had been severed. He was screaming for a cigarette.

Edwin was on call that night and when he arrived at the scene was astounded to find his niece one of the injured. Along with others who were hurt he drove her to the hospital and then phoned Grannie and Grandad to tell them what had happened.

Clare was young and strong and appeared to recover quickly from the accident. The muscles around the damaged disc in her back compensated. But she was always in pain from the blow to her jaw and it was not until years later, when her back was under stress during childbirth, that the severity of her back injury was discovered.

Mother had not been feeling well for several weeks.

"Will you please do the shopping for me today, Annette?" she asked one Saturday. "I just don't feel up to it. I'll make you a list."

I went to the drawer where the ration books were kept and there was a green book entitling the holder to extra milk and eggs.

"What's this? I thought green books were for pregnant women."

"That's right. I'm pregnant."

At sixteen I was appalled. How could my mother be pregnant at her age? Mother had a difficult time throughout her pregnancy and spent a lot of time in bed. Clare and I did what we could to help, taking on the household chores and doing the shopping after school.

In October, 1947, Edwin was born, a late 'demob' baby for Mother and Dad but one of thousands born that year to returning servicemen. He had three adoring, ready-made surrogate mothers and did not lack for attention. But Mother was forty-one and the last thing she wanted was a new baby. She was exhausted after holding everything together for years. She felt that Dad's 'war' had been much easier than hers. And before the war even began she'd had five difficult years in the ghastly fish shop at Loampit Vale. She felt trapped.

Everything was closing in on her. She held Dad totally responsible for her problems.

When it came time to name the baby, Dad wanted to call him Edward but Mother was adamant that he not have the same name.

"It's too confusing when father and son have the same name. Look how it's been with the Coppards - all those Georges - and you and your father both Edward. And then Aunt Constance and Connie. I want to call him Edwin."

Edwin, her brother, had always been held up as a paragon of virtue, a handyman, with whom Dad could never hope to compete. The fact that there would be another duplication of names with two Edwins in the family did not seem to occur to her. Then we girls entered the fray, siding with Mother. For some reason we thought that Edwin was a romantic name. And so Dad was defeated. Dorothy's husband, Guy, another successful man, was to be the godfather and therefore the baby was named Edwin Guy.

As soon as Dad got home from work, Mother would start picking on him and there were constant, awful arguments. Many of their rows were over lack of money. The fish stall was not doing so well.

"If you'd got that instructor's qualification you'd have a good job now," Mother would shout.

Sometimes on a Friday night Dad asked,

"Shall we go to the pictures tonight, Alice?"

"No, I'm too tired."

Then on Saturday she'd say,

"Let's go to the pictures, Annette."

But I refused to be a husband substitute and almost always refused. So she was displeased with me, too.

Dad's life was no easier than hers, but Mother bitterly resented the time he spent running. She was hostile to his hope of running a marathon. He indulged himself for a few hours each week while she was stuck. Her discontent and despondency cast a pall of unhappiness and unease over us all. Clare managed to escape. She found herself a job with a veterinary surgeon and left home. This was the beginning of what became a very successful business breeding her own dogs. I was soon to leave for college but Jennifer cried herself to sleep every night.

The National Health Service came into effect in July, 1948. No longer did anyone have to pay directly for health, dental or optical services.

"When are you going to get new glasses, Dad?" asked Jennifer.

Dad's glasses were decidedly the worse for wear. He, Mother and I, all short-sighted, made appointments with the optician to get new glasses now that they were free.

In the summer of 1948 I was lucky to be one of a group of girls from school to travel to Sweden. The money I had saved from my paper route was not enough so Grandad made up what was needed. We travelled overland from the south of France, through Germany and so on to Sweden. The bomb damage in London was awful enough, I had thought, but I stared aghast as the train travelled by what seemed like mile after mile of rubble in Germany.

I travelled from Stockholm a day's train ride to Örnsköldsvik, just below the Arctic Circle, so far north that in summer the sun never sets all night. The summer home of the family with whom I stayed was on a little inlet and here I spent the holiday enjoying the swimming and boating, but most of all, the food.

At my first lunch I gazed in astonishment at the laden table: a great slab of butter, several kinds of cheese, sandwiches of every description, bowls of fruit and a great pitcher of cream. I was introduced to a variety of new foods: 'open' sandwiches, crayfish, pancakes with lingonberry sauce, all of which I loved. My hosts must have thought me very greedy as I devoured everything I was offered.

One day, sour Baltic herring was served, which I politely declined. The smell of it was so pungent that I didn't even want to be in the same room with it.

"This is very strong, Annette. We won't be offended if you don't eat it," said my host, in impeccable English, "in fact, after we've finished eating we take the dishes down to the creek and soak them overnight to get the smell out before we wash them!"

In subsequent years we enjoyed having the son and daughter of the family stay with us on their visits to England.

While I was still in Sweden, Britain hosted the first Olympic Games to be held since 1936. They were called the 'austerity Olympics' because no new stadiums were built and there was nothing ostentatious. Dad took Jennifer to Wembley Stadium where the athletics were held. At the age of eleven, she fell in love for the first time - with Arthur Wint, the Jamaican sprinter. He flowed along the track. She was entranced.

"What did you think of that?"

"Oh, Dad, he was wonderful."

From that seminal moment, it was a natural progression for Jennifer to become involved in sports and develop a highly successful career.

Then Draper Street was closed to street traders and Dad was out of work. He set about finding a job, something he'd never had to do before. A job as salesman in a fish shop lasted a few months. But he hated working for someone who knew less about the business than he did. He quit and started looking for something else.

He applied for work at a sheet-metal factory where he was asked,

"Can you operate a guillotine?"

All that he'd ever read about a guillotine was in the context of the French Revolution.

"Show me and I'll tell you if I can manage it."

The foreman took him over to where a man was using the shear. Dad scrutinized the procedure intently.

"Yes, I can handle that."

"Can you read a rule?"

" 'course I can read a bloody rule. Where do you think I was brought up?"

Dad was hired.

There was still a shortage of steel and so great gasometers, stinking of coal gas, were brought into the factory to be hammered and flattened into six by four panels, thousands and thousands of them. It was punishing work. When the big smelting mills were closed, new six by four sheets of steel came into the factory to be cut into three by twos. As he cut the sheets Dad admired the beautiful blue gloss on the metal. But then the Liverpool shipyards began to close, the steel was no longer wanted and everything shut down. Dad was out of a job again. Once more he had to look for employment. Like most men of his generation, Dad had a tremendous work ethic and was despondent when he couldn't find a well-paying job.

Birthday Party, June, 1951

Back: Edward, Annette, Clare, Howard (Connies, h.), Paul (Clare's h.), Connie, Bobby, Phyllis (Edwin's w.), Dorothy, Constance, Edwin (Alice's b.)
Middle: Jennifer, Grandad, Grannie, Edwin (on knee), Alice
Front: Sukey, Antony (Dorothy's son), Sheila (Edwin's d.), Jill (Edwin's d.), Christopher (Dorothy's s.), Rosemary (Edwin's d.)

MARATHON RUNNING

It's a very private thing, running. Most of the time it's a solitary thing. I'd always dreamed of running a marathon and I had to do it before I was too old. I didn't have a trainer. What I really needed was someone to have pulled me out on my ten mile practice runs.

After demobilization, Dad renewed his association with the Kent Athletic Club and started running again. He began to dream of doing a marathon. Cross-country runners, with the support of their various clubs, were beginning to show an interest in the marathon.

In keeping with his forbears - his grandfather swimming around Brighton Pier, his father sprinting up the steps of the Monument - Dad was displaying a certain flair, if not flamboyance, in running the marathon at a time when very few people did. His sister, Dorothy, with her long-distance swimming and water polo exploits, certainly belonged in this company of athletic family eccentrics.

The Windsor to London marathon which Dad aspired to enter was, in effect, the Olympic trials. The field was élite; the best runners in the country ran in this race. The strict entry qualification required each competitor to have run a marathon in under three hours or a twenty mile race in under two and a half hours. In addition, he had to be a member of a club. These qualifying races were held two months before the marathon to show that a runner was in good form at the time of the race.

The Amateur Athletic Association twenty mile race, run under strict rules, was the qualifying national championship for the marathon. Another qualifying race was the Finchley Harriers tough twenty mile, considered a 'runner's' course. In both of these races Dad ran a time of less than two hours fifteen minutes.

In those days, running a marathon didn't take over your life. Dad followed the accepted methods of training of that time. Three days a week after work he made his way to a track where he'd warm up and then run as fast as he could for ten miles before heading for home. Other days he came straight home and did an evening run with Sukey. With his tall, spare build, Dad had an easy, loping stride.

Sunday mornings he would have three or four raw eggs beaten up in a glass of milk before setting off for a twenty-five mile run with Sukey for company. The distance she covered was more like thirty miles because she constantly took side trips to investigate interesting smells. For a year before his first marathon in 1948, Dad ran about seventy miles a week, gradually reducing his time over the long run from four to three hours.

He always followed the same route away from the house - up Copse Avenue, along Woodland Way, through Threehalfpenny Wood to the Addington golf courses, around which he often ran, ignoring *Keep Out* signs. Sometimes he ran further afield. Usually he finished with a stop at the *Cricketers* where he indulged in a beer and got water for Sukey before the last run up Spout Hill and home. For a few weeks before the date of the race, three other men from the K.A.C. team joined him on Sundays for the run and then they'd all return with enormous appetites for a big lunch.

On our street Dad had garnered a certain notoriety.

"That's the man who runs. He takes his dog, too, you know."

In West Wickham no one else went out running. Walking and cycling were acceptable, indeed commonplace, but not running. After the manner of teenagers everywhere, we girls would have no part of this aberrant behaviour in a parent. It was a while before we came to appreciate and respect Dad's tremendous endeavour.

Mother complained that he did not spend enough time with Edwin, so one day he left on his run with Edwin seated on his shoulders. But this was not repeated since Edwin had not taken kindly to the bouncing motion.

Dad's credit in the neighbourhood was further eroded after an episode with Patch, a neighbourhood dog always on the loose. Patch's coat was a dirty white, splattered with irregular patches of black and brown. One ear flopped, the result of a fight; the other stood upright. Around his left eye was a black patch. He was the epitome of mongrel. Moreover he had fathered most of the unwanted dog population in West Wickham and was universally hated.

Sukey had delivered her third litter of Patch's pups some months previously. It was difficult to find homes for all the puppies and now that she was on heat again, we were careful to keep her in. Apart from the problem of unwanted progeny, a pregnancy would slow down Dad's running partner.

Sukey slept in a kennel in the back garden. Dad, whose bedroom overlooked the garden, woke early one morning to the sound of excited yelps from Sukey, punctuated by loud crashing sounds.

"It's that bloody Patch!"

Dad leapt out of bed, rushed down to the kitchen, and flung open the back door. Patch was throwing himself bodily against the fence, trying to get to Sukey. The fence was flimsy enough without this kind of punishment. With each assault it buckled, and the noise from the impact ricocheted along the neighbours' fences. People came to their doors to see what all the racket was about.

There was a rending sound, a piece of the fence fell into the garden, and Patch's head appeared. Grabbing a poker, Dad leapt out of the door and made for the back gate. He heaved it open and Patch took off pursued by Dad in pyjamas, barefoot, brandishing his poker. But Patch was a sprinter and easily outpaced the marathon runner.

In 1908, the Polytechnic Harriers had organized the first marathon race to be run from Windsor to London. Each succeeding year the race, often started by a member of the Royal Family who took a special interest in the marathon, set off from the private grounds of Windsor Castle. Swinging through the town of Windsor, the course continued up the Great North Road to the grounds of Polytechnic Harriers. Other routes were followed during some years of the two World Wars, but in 1946 the original Windsor to London route resumed.

On Saturday, June 19, 1948, Dad ran his first marathon, representing the Kent Athletic Club. He was forty-three. He had worked all week as usual. The morning of the race he walked the mile to the station, took the train to London and then another train to Windsor. From the station he walked briskly towards the Castle in time for the race at 3:30 p.m. Windsor Castle, built by William the Conqueror, is west of London, on the River Thames. Dad had not been to Windsor since he and Mother had taken a trip there before they were married.

The area to which he now made his way was only opened to the public for special events such as the marathon. Dad identified himself and was directed towards the stables. Space had been made available in the stables for competitors to change. These were no ordinary stables; they housed not merely horses but all the trappings and paraphernalia for royal pageants. He would have liked time to examine closely the big shields with coats of arms, and the coaches. These were things he'd seen only from a distance before as he'd stood to watch a parade pass by.

Dad changed into his shorts and a singlet with wide horizontal stripes, put on his running shoes and made his way into the Quadrangle from where the race was to start. Two hundred and fifteen competitors were jogging about, warming up, waiting for the officials and Queen Elizabeth to make an appearance. Then they lined up to be presented. The Queen, accompanied by the King, walked down the rows of the assembled competitors, shaking hands, speaking a few words.

The Queen addressed Dad:

"Have you run this marathon before?"

"No, Ma'am, this is my first marathon race."

Her Majesty turned to another runner.

"Where are you from?"

"Leeds, Ma'am."

"How are you getting back?"

"In an ambulance, probably, Ma'am."

Everyone laughed and the tension eased a little.

The Queen, as the official starter, fired the gun, and they were off, under the archway, out of the close. In the route laid out in the programme, the names of pubs, easily identified landmarks, featured prominently as mileage markers:

Jolly Butchers - 4 ¾ miles;

Crooked Billett - 9 ½ miles;

Red Lion - 10 ½ miles

Tower Arms - 12 ½ miles.

In any event it would have been impossible to stray off course with runners in front, runners behind and people cheering them on.

The *Rising Sun* at nineteen miles loomed in view. Dad was tenth in the field. He put on the pressure and pulled ahead. But then he had an attack of diarrhea and dropped to the side. When he reentered the field there was no way he could make up the lost time.

The last six miles were hell, needles of pain as each foot hit the ground, one foot after the other, on and on. In a haze of pain and fatigue he persisted, every inch of the twenty-six miles, three hundred and eighty-five yards, to the end, completing the race with a lap around Chiswick Stadium. He finished forty-fourth with a time of three hours exactly. Jack Holden of the Tipton Harriers won the marathon in a time of two hours, thirty-six minutes.

At the end of the race some of the runners were in very bad shape, especially those who hadn't trained properly and had pushed themselves too hard. Huge tubs of water were provided for contestants to bathe in. As some of the men slid unconscious under the water, St. John's Ambulance attendants were on hand to haul them to the surface and revive them.

Dad bathed and dressed and started on his way home. He was so tired he could hardly walk. Arriving at Waterloo Station he headed to the bar to await his train home.

"Double Scotch, please."

"What d'you want in it?"

"Nothing."

He tossed it back.

"Another of the same, please."

For his third drink he had a single.

The train drew in to the station and Dad dragged himself on board. When he got off the train at West Wickham he could barely crawl the mile home. Had there been such a thing as a taxi he might have taken it.

For five consecutive years Dad ran the Windsor to London marathon but never equalled the time of his first race.

Christmas, 1957

Annette, Clare, Jennifer, Edwin, Edward, Alice

EMIGRATION

I was in a state of flux. There had to be something better for me but I wondered if I'd have the courage. The courage to leave everything behind and come to Canada. After all I was nearly fifty and the only thing I knew was the fish business.

Dad wrote to me:

'I'm glad you're getting the chance to go to college. You'll always have a good job. My father should have given me the opportunity to continue my education, but he took me out of school when I was fourteen. I always resented that.'

In September of 1948, I had gone away to one of the several colleges built in the immediate post-war years to address the shortage of teachers.

Gradually life in Britain lightened. Clothes rationing came to an end in 1949, although food shortages continued. The bill of fare at my college contained very little protein and on Guy Fawkes Day we burned our college mascot, Carbohydrate Clara, in effigy on the top of the bonfire.

It was not until 1954 that the last food item, meat, was derationed. Then a ceremonial tearing up of ration books took place in Trafalgar Square.

On leaving college, I got my first teaching job. I was glad to be able to contribute to the family income, although as a beginning female teacher I was paid less than a man for the same job. To my disgust I discovered that a road sweeper was paid more than I was.

The Festival of Britain was opened by the King in May, 1951. Twenty-seven acres of cleared bomb sites on London's South Bank were used for buildings to house the exhibits and other attractions. The director of the festival, Herbert Morrison, thought that one of its main purposes should be to dispel the gloom caused by continuing postwar austerities. And this it did. Along with millions of people from all over Great Britain we made our way through the exhibits, enjoyed the fun fair, and went to concerts in the new Royal Festival Hall.

In June, Mother organized a family party for my twenty-first birthday. The occasion for the celebration was my birthday but it was much more than that. For the first time since the war had begun, both sides of the family were able to get together. The Ansteys - Grannie and Grandad, Uncle Edwin, his wife and their three girls. And all the Coppards - Aunt Constance, Bobby, and Connie and Dorothy with their respective husbands and children. The cousins were introduced to each other. Jennifer, fourteen, in the awkward place between child and adult, was delegated to look after the young fry, much to her annoyance. Clare and I joined the adults. Finally I was officially of age. Someone produced a camera and we took group photos, with Grannie and Grandad, the elders, in the middle. Altogether it was a great day.

The following year we celebrated Clare's special birthday and then, in December, her wedding. Jennifer and I were bridesmaids. Clare was an excellent seamstress and made all the dresses herself. It was the first wedding in the family and she proudly made all the arrangements herself. Clare had the distinction of being married by the Reverend Ramsay, who went on to become Archbishop of Canterbury.

I joined a group of young people who got together every weekend. We gathered in each others' houses to listen to records. We enjoyed London life, going to plays and concerts. Once we went to the Promenade Concerts at the Royal Albert Hall every night for a week of Beethoven. For a shilling, which I could just afford, concert-goers stood or sat on the floor in the arena. Sir Thomas Beecham was conducting. One evening, a young woman beside us fainted and there was a commotion while she was carried out. The music stopped. Looking towards us plebians standing below him, Beecham intoned,

"If there are any other young ladies thinking of swooning, would they please stand near the fountain so that they may be instantly revived?"

Everyone laughed and the concert resumed.

As a member of a big London choir, I took part in some exciting performances. In the first recorded performance of Carl Orff's *Carmina Burana*, Alfred Deller was the counter-tenor. Following the score, my friend Joyce and I knew that it was almost time for Deller's entry but he was nowhere in sight. The people in the recording booth were becoming agitated. We looked at each other.

"What'll they do if he doesn't show up?" I whispered to Joyce.

At that moment Deller, tall, black-bearded, very masculine, strolled in, opened his mouth and sang his spine-tingling high notes.

Suddenly, Aunt Constance, everyone's favourite aunt, died. She had been with us for Christmas but, afraid that she had cancer, told no one that she was in great pain. When she was finally taken to hospital in February, it was too late. A bleeding stomach ulcer killed her. On the day of her funeral the weather was as bleak as my heart. I wanted another chance to tell Aunt Constance how much I had loved her kindness and what she had meant to me.

A public holiday was declared for the big event of June 2, 1953, the coronation of Queen Elizabeth. This was the first time such a ceremony had been televised. People were generous and asked neighbours without televisions into their homes to watch. My friend's aunt invited me to her home where twelve of us huddled around her television set to see Queen Elizabeth crowned in Westminster Abbey.

The housing shortage after the war was acute. During the war some two hundred thousand houses had been blown up or burnt down. In addition a quarter of a million houses were so badly damaged they were uninhabitable and another quarter of a million were severely damaged. To address the immediate crisis of homeless people, prefabricated houses were built.

New Addington was a town of prefabs created after the war for homeless people. The factory-made prefabicated houses were quickly put together on site and erected to create instant towns. Each of the families in the prefabs had at least two children and the schools built to accommodate them were immediately filled.

After taking a year out to study music, I began teaching at one of the New Addington schools. Four miles from Croydon, one of the most heavily bombed areas in the London area, exposed and windy at the top of a hill, New Addington was known as Little Siberia. By the time I had walked on a winter's day from the bus stop to the school my face was so cold I could barely speak.

But while new opportunities seemed to be opening up for

all of us, life for Dad had not improved. He continued to have a series of low-paying, awful jobs which he hated. There did not seem to be any opportunity for him in England although there were fewer people dependent on him. Clare was married, I was teaching, and much to Mother's delight, Jennifer was headed to college to become a physical education teacher.

"There's no future for me here," he lamented.

Dad was despondent. He became restless. In him grew the prospective immigrant's profound dissatisfaction with his present life and the hope for something better in a new land.

He was not the first Coppard maverick to think of emigrating. Three of Dad's first cousins also left England. The first was George Maynard Coppard's son, George Herbert, who went to New Zealand in 1926. His family joined him later. Emily Coppard's son, Frank Smith, emigrated to Canada in 1948. And Frank Coppard's son, Douglas, moved to Australia in 1957.

In the next generation, Dorothy Coppard's son, Anthony Creak, started a new life in Australia in 1972.

At our local library Dad took out everything he could find on Canada and Alaska. He was fascinated by accounts of giant Alaska King Crab being stretched out on the surface of the ice and frozen with their long legs extended. He wanted to see that for himself. The immense size of Great Slave Lake on the map of Canada impressed him.

In the evenings, Dad, the mandatory cup of tea at his elbow, pored over books and maps and pamphlets. On the other side of the table sat Jennifer, with her school books in front of her, ostensibly doing homework. I would bring my most prized twenty-first birthday present, a gramophone which Grandad had given me, and play one of my records. Dad had a good voice and sang the folk songs along with

Peter Pears. Even though he had had no formal training, Dad discovered an affinity for classical music.

"What's that you're playing?"

"It's Mozart."

"I like it. Get some more of him."

Any spare money I had was spent on records.

Finally he set his sights on Canada.

"But what will you do there, Dad?" asked Jennifer.

"I think I'd be able to get a job on the West Coast. I'll start with Prince Rupert - big fishing industry there."

"When I've finished college, maybe I can get a job there, too."

Dad began to get excited. His gloom gradually lifted. His plan was to get himself established and then send for Mother and Edwin. He wrote to a friend of Dorothy's in Edmonton, an R.C.A.F. man she had kept in touch with since he'd been in England during the war.

John wrote back.

'Come and visit. We'd love to see you. You can travel on to Prince Rupert easily from here. But forget about Great Slave Lake. It'll be frozen solid for a while yet.'

"I'll take a boat to Montreal," said Dad. "I want to see Montreal and Quebec City. Fascinating history."

"How far is it from Montreal to Prince Rupert?" I asked him.

"Don't you know anything about Canada?"

"No idea. Remember I only ever studied Australia?"

"From east to west it's about five thousand miles. It takes several days to travel across the country by train. But I guess that the huge distance won't sink in until I'm actually sitting in the train watching the miles go by. In area, Canada is forty times bigger than Great Britain although most of it is uninhabited."

Dad applied to emigrate and went to Canada House in

Trafalgar Square for his medical examination and chest x-ray. There was a problem. Apparently Dad's x-ray showed a scar on his left lung. He was called back to see the doctor.

"There's what appears to be an old scar on your lung. Was there ever tuberculosis in your family?" asked the doctor.

"My family was decimated by it," said Dad, "my mother, two sisters, a baby brother, an aunt and cousins. They all died."

"Then it's very likely that you yourself had the disease. We'd like to have more x-rays and take some tests. Then we'll call you."

When Dad returned a few days later the doctor spoke to him.

"We've looked at all the x-rays. Considering your family's history it seems probable that the scar we see is the result of your having had tuberculosis yourself as a child.

But you were lucky - the lung healed itself. After recovering from tuberculosis a person's lungs show a few calcified spots on an x-ray. The tests show that it is certainly not active and we can give you a clean bill of health."

Finally, everything was in order for Dad to emigrate to Canada. He got his passport. In the space where it asked for occupation, he wrote: *Fishmonger.*

In the spring of 1955 the *Columbia* was the first boat to sail up the St. Lawrence into Montreal. In April of that year, just one month before his fiftieth birthday, my father took passage on the *Columbia* and emigrated to Canada.

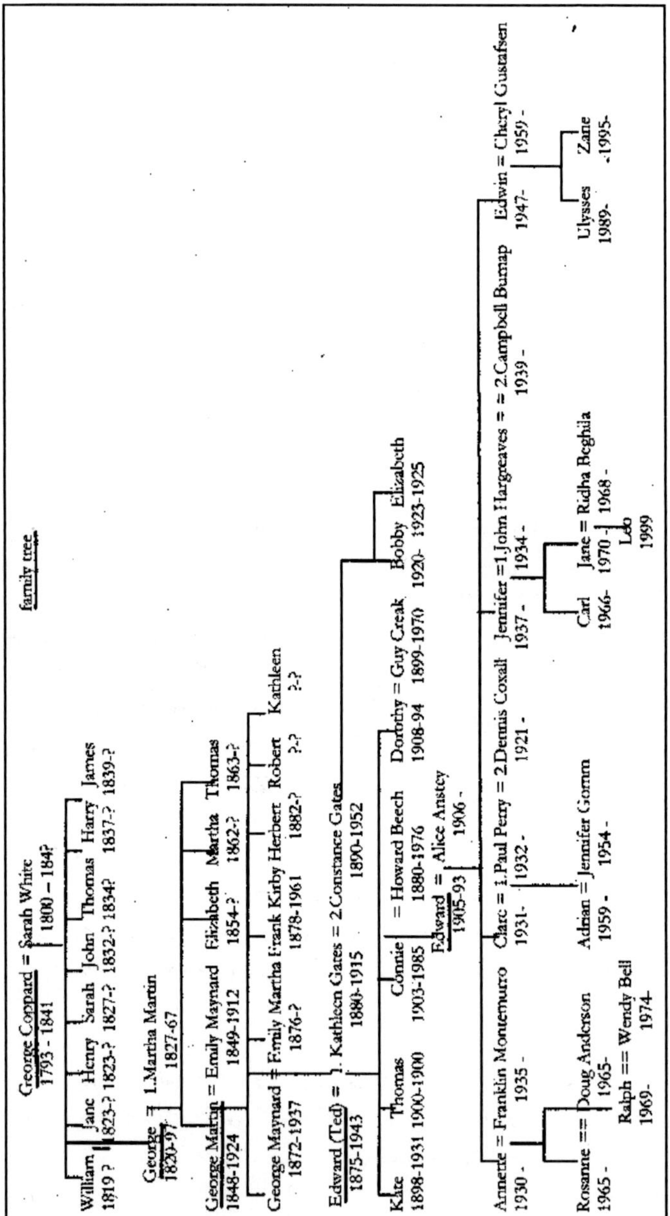

family tree
George Coppard = Sarah White
1793 - 1841
1800 – 184?
William 1819 ?
Jane 1823-?
Henry 1823-?
Sarah 1827-?
John 1832-?
Thomas 1834?
Harry 1837-?
James 1839-?
George 1820-97
= 1.Martha Martin 1827-67
George Martin 1848-1924
= Emily Maynard 1849-1912
Elizabeth 1854-?
Martha 1862-?
Thomas 1863-?
George Maynard 1872-1937
Emily Martha 1876-?
Frank Kirby 1878-1961
Herbert 1882-?
Robert ?-?
Kathleen ?-?
Edward (Ted) 1875-1943
= 1. Kathleen Gates 1880-1915
= 2.Constance Gates 1890-1952
Kate 1898-1931
Thomas 1900-1900
Connie 1903-1985
= Howard Beech 1880-1976
Dorothy 1908-94
= Guy Creak 1899-1970
Bobby 1920-
Elizabeth 1923-1925
Edward 1905-93
= Alice Anstey 1906 -
Annette 1930 -
= Franklin Montemurro 1935 -
Clare 1931-
= 1.Paul Perry 1932 -
= 2.Dennis Coxall 1921 -
Jennifer 1937 -
=1.John Hargreaves 1934 -
= = 2.Campbell Burnap 1939 -
Edwin 1947-
= Cheryl Gustafsen 1959 -
Rosanne 1965 -
== Doug Anderson 1965-
Ralph 1969-
== Wendy Bell 1974
Adrian 1959 -
= Jennifer Gomm 1954 -
Carl 1966-
Jane 1970 -
= Ridha Beghila 1968 -
Leo 1999
Ulysses 1989-
Zane 1995-

postscript

After landing in Montreal in April of 1955, Edward Coppard travelled by train across Canada to Prince Rupert where his first job was grading halibut on a fishing boat. He was fired the same day for placing the wrong size fish in a bin.

In return for doing odd jobs, Dad obtained free passage on a boat travelling to Vancouver where he took a room for $7.00 a week and started looking for work. He took any job he could find: plumber's helper, sheet-metal worker, construction worker.

When in November of 1956, it was feared that England would be at war with Egypt over the Suez Canal, Dad returned to England. The crisis over, he went back to Canada where he worked on the West Coast of Vancouver Island. After another brief trip back to England, Dad decided that Canada was where he wanted to be. In early 1959, he sailed again to Montreal where he worked for several months before making his way to Vancouver.

I had begun teaching in Vancouver the year before. When Dad arrived we rented an apartment together where Mother joined us.

Mother came into her own - getting involved in environmental causes and social issues. She loved having the opportunity to travel extensively as representative of various groups. In conjunction with the United Nations' Association in Canada, the City of Vancouver conferred on her the Citizen Peace Award in 1993.

Edwin completed his schooling in Vancouver, and is an accomplished songwriter/musician and teacher.

Clare developed a successful business and enjoys travelling extensively to show and judge pedigree dogs.

Jennifer is a well-known professor of sport sociology and was one of the early pioneers in that field.

In 1960 Dad qualified as a Red Cross Water Safety Instructor and then obtained an Industrial First Aid Certificate and a bookkeeping credential which enabled him to make a good living. He travelled to remote logging camps and came to know and love British Columbia.

When he retired Dad was able once again to indulge his love of running and tennis. He learned to play golf and would set off from home on his bicycle pulling his golf cart behind him. He took advantage of seniors' concessions on the local golf course where, to the dismay of the marshal, he would often spend the whole day.

Dad renewed contact with his cousins and exchanged visits with them: George Herbert Coppard in New Zealand, George Smith in Toronto and Doug Coppard and Dorothy's son, Anthony, in Australia.

Cousins of later generations also came to know each other. Clare's and Jennifer's children were frequent visitors to Canada. 'Gramps' had a special relationship with each of his grandchildren who formed a rapt audience for his continuing stories: being chased out of town by a sheriff in Ontario because he looked scruffy; flying in single-engine planes so overloaded they barely got off the ground....

Edward Coppard died on Boxing Day, 1993.

about the author

Annette Montemurro was born and educated in Great Britain. As a child at the outbreak of World War II, she was evacuated from the London area to a small village in Sussex. After her return to London she and her family lived through the Blitz and the Flying Bombs.

In 1958, she accepted a teaching position in Vancouver and went on to complete her degree at U.B.C.

Following her father's death in 1993 the author transcribed his recorded memoirs and undertook extensive research in the U.K to verify the facts. She made contact with several members of the Coppard clan in Canada, England, Australia and New Zealand. Her passion for letter writing enabled her to garner details from them to embellish the story.

Annette Montemurro lives with her husband in Coquitlam, British Columbia.